I am always looking for practical books about managing people to recommend. This book is full of common sense and is at the top of my list!

Elizabeth Toogood, Toogood Critical Friend
www.ToogoodCriticalFriend.co.uk

This book can help you whether you are new to managing people or have been doing it for years. There are tips, insights and practical information that tell you the essentials of what you really need to know. They will help you to demystify the challenges of working out why people do what they do, and what you can do to build an effective team. I highly recommend this book to anyone who manages individuals on a day-to-day basis.

Peter Gibbons, Managing Director, Genius
www.GeniusConsultancy.co.uk

I've had the privilege of working very closely with Michelle, and benefitting from her knowledge and expertise first hand. As a new manager, Michelle's experience has helped make my transition into management seamless. This book captures Michelle's expertise perfectly and makes helpful reading for managers at all levels.

Jade Croucher, Operations Manager, The Open Data Institute
www.TheODI.org

The book is clear, helpful and strikes a good balance between being a 'how to' and being a general overview.

Polly Gavins, Polly Gavins Ltd
www.PollyGavins.co.uk

Acknowledgements

I could not have written this book if it was not for the wonderful marketing skills of Chantal Cornelius.

I first met Chantal at a networking seminar soon after setting up my People Management business. For some years now Chantal and her team at Appletree have been looking after my marketing and I have been kept busy with work!

One of the aspects of the Marketing Plan Chantal devised for me was a regular series of newsletters that enabled me to discuss a variety of People Management subjects. In the newsletters I shared my learning and experience gained from studying for Human Resources (HR) and Organisational Development (OD) qualifications and from over twenty-five years of working in People Management.

At one of our meetings to discuss the newsletters, Chantal said, "You should write a book." After a bit of cajoling and encouragement, I eventually started to write. Chantal has been wonderfully supportive during the whole process, reassuring me that what I have to say is relevant and would be of interest to an audience. She has shown limitless patience in the face of numerous changes, the occasional crisis of confidence and seemingly endless edits – thank you Chantal!

My thanks also go to those who have contributed, critiqued, encouraged and generously given their time to help make sense of my thoughts and words.

Contents

START HERE

I have been working in the field of People Management for over twenty-five years. In that time I have been a manager and I have been managed. The benefit of learning and experience from both sides has proved invaluable when advising clients how to successfully meet their People Management needs.

Whether you are experienced or are new to People Management, my aim for this book is to provide you with insights, reassurance and ideas about what you really need to make your life as a manager of people more productive and successful. It will also serve as a useful reference point to deal with a difficult issue, or when you have an idea for doing something different in your organisation.

This book is not a textbook that tells you everything there is to know about the day-to-day practical and theoretical aspects of HR or OD. There are many excellent books out there on these subjects and a number of these are referenced at the end of this book. Similarly there are a number of websites that provide extensive details of employment law and aspects of HR that an employer should be following.

This book is a collection of insights into what managing people really entails. One such insight is that no textbook, research paper or established process will provide you with a guaranteed perfect solution to every challenge that working with people will throw at you. You and every one of the people you work alongside are unique human beings and there are no perfect answers when it comes to managing them.

The amount of information available on the subject of People Management is huge and covers a vast array of opinions and advice. In this book I look at the fundamental aspects of People Management that will help you establish the building blocks for managing and developing an effective team. It also provides pointers to the research, theories and thinking that underpin these fundamental aspects.

This book examines how, as the Boss, you can impact on your teams and how you can plan your People Management strategy. There are also chapters describing the key elements of how to build a high performing team.

An important feature of the book is Five Key Factors I have seen employed by successful managers and business owners. Despite having very different personalities, these people all share a common approach to effective People Management that can be distilled into the Five Key Factors.

In each chapter I identify how the Five Key Factors apply to the subject matter and how you can use these to develop a successful approach to People Management. I will reference them at the end of the chapters of this book to illustrate how they apply.

As with any endeavour, it is important to build from the correct foundations. Therefore, each chapter in this book sets out 'A Good Place To Start' on the subject it will cover. Each chapter also concludes with a summary of essential elements that can be used as a reference point as you continue along your People Management journey.

In the years I have been helping clients resolve People Management issues and challenges I have found that whilst the approaches used to tackle them are similar, the detail of each case is different. Even now when I am helping clients with a People Management problem I am often astonished at the capacity that human beings have to surprise us. I often find myself using the expression:

"The only predictable thing about people is that they are unpredictable."

This is usually in response to an exasperated manager who has asked why a situation with an employee has arisen, why the employee has behaved in such a way or how someone may react in a particular situation.

Early on in my career I realised that it is impossible to accurately predict what people will do or how they will react. This does not mean that it is impossible to effectively manage the people you work with.

People Management is easier to do if you carefully think about your approach, including anticipating and preparing for a wide range of employees' personalities. As I have already mentioned, people are unique and will bring different ambitions, needs, frustrations, strengths and foibles to work with them. However, properly managed, you can use these unique characteristics to form part of your competitive advantage.

The first challenge for anyone who manages one person, or an organisation that employs thousands, is to recognise that a proactive approach to People Management is as much a priority as managing finance, marketing, sales and all the other functions that make an organisation successful. You may think that I would say that because that's my business. However, the reason I am saying it is because I have seen the human and financial cost of poor People Management that negatively impacts on individuals, teams and the whole organisation. I have also seen the positive impact that a high performing team can have on increasing productivity and making work an enjoyable place to be.

I can't promise you a quick fix 'People Management Made Easy' toolkit. Learning any subject, including People Management, is achieved through a combination of being taught, teaching yourself and applied experience. Perhaps most of all, it is through understanding the lessons from when we get it wrong as much as when we get it right.

CHAPTER ONE

PEOPLE MANAGEMENT

At some point you will have decided whether to work in splendid isolation, or if you will follow a vocation that involves working with other people.

As you are reading this book we'll assume that you decided on the latter, and that you want to build a successful career whereby the management of people, in some shape or form, is likely to become a regular aspect of your working life.

People Management can be enjoyable, frustrating, rewarding, exasperating, unpleasant, fun, upsetting, confusing and inspiring, all in the same day. The enjoyable includes taking a chance on hiring and training someone and then seeing them develop a successful career. The frustrating includes having to deal with relatively minor issues such as "he said, she said" petty squabbles. The upsetting can include an employee's personal or health issues and the unpleasant will include grievances, disciplinaries and dismissals. These are all the things that come with any role involving the management of people that are not usually referred to in a job description.

To become a successful manager of people, a greater understanding and awareness of the subject of People Management will help you.

'MANAGING PEOPLE' AND 'PEOPLE MANAGEMENT': WHAT'S THE DIFFERENCE?

In this book, the context of 'managing people' covers all the practical aspects of employing people, including paperwork, processes and legalities from recruitment through to when employment ends.

As I have mentioned in the introduction to this book, there are many readily available sources of good information that will help you with the minutiae of the practices and processes of managing people. This book focuses on the broader elements of the fundamentals that can help you to develop an awareness and understanding of 'People Management'.

I see People Management as a strategy for identifying and utilising a range of approaches to maximise the unique opportunity you have to develop your organisation via the people you employ.

A proactive People Management strategy acknowledges that people are individuals and that a 'one size fits all' approach is not the most effective way to get the best out of everyone in your team. It also acknowledges that there are no magic formulas or quick fixes when dealing with people.

Developing your learning and understanding about why people do what they do will help you to build an effective People Management strategy.

A GOOD PLACE TO START:
SEVEN ESSENTIALS OF PEOPLE MANAGEMENT

As a starting point for developing your people strategy, I am going to share seven essentials that I have identified and frequently relate to clients about People Management:

1. The only predictable thing about people is that they are unpredictable

This is a phrase that I often use with exasperated managers who are trying to understand an employee's behaviour. Whilst it is not possible to second-guess exactly what people will do, it is possible to consider different scenarios and how you might deal with them.

A useful tip is to not presume individuals will react in a predictable way. I learnt this lesson from one of my early experiences of having to give employees the bad news of redundancies. I had prepared for those people I thought would be distraught, only to find myself surprised when they weren't. Conversely, the apparently self-confident people who were then inconsolable equally surprised me.

One of the traps of People Management that I often see managers falling into is assuming that all the members of their team will think, feel and react the same way that they themselves would do in a given situation. They are often frustrated when someone doesn't agree with, appreciate or see something in the same way that they do.

Human beings, and remember that includes you, are unique and whilst there may be similarities in personalities and approach, don't assume that what you would do is what someone else will do. The over used phrase about 'assume' making 'an ass of you and me' is very often true with People Management.

2. One size does not fit all

Teams are a collection of individuals, all of whom are unique. Factors including their personality, the reasons why they are working, and why they work for you, will differ from person to person.

This means that taking a People Management approach that presumes everyone will think and behave in exactly the same way will not work. This also applies if you take the same approach to the same scenario with different people. For example, two people may be doing the same job with a similar level of knowledge, skills and experience. However, one may be able to work with minimal direction whilst the other performs better when given more support in task setting and checking.

Whilst it doesn't mean doing everything completely differently for every person you employ, it does mean some aspects of your overall approach may require adjustment.

One size does not fit all when it also comes to processes. I am not saying that if you introduce a process you need to develop something that is individually tailored to each person. When planning any process think about how it can be flexible to better suit the needs of individuals and therefore, your organisation.

3. *Change is inevitable and isn't always planned*

Think about your life and the factors that have led you to where you are today. A number of aspects will have been planned, such as going to school, deciding on a choice of career or targeting an organisation you want to work for. Many more of them will have been unplanned, including meeting and falling for someone who lives miles away from you, or making a choice about a job due to the health and welfare of yourself or someone significant to you.

Just as you experience changes in your life, think of all of the things that will be changing in other people's lives.

Striving for nirvana in respect of the work you do and the team that you work with is a great goal. But remember that if you expect to reach a point when you can sit back and watch things tick over successfully in the same way for many months or years, you are going to be disappointed.

If in striving for nirvana you appreciate that you will need to be flexible and prepared to plan for or react to changes, then you will be more successful.

I often hear the phrase 'people fear change.' What I find is not that people fear change, but that they fear the unknowns associated with change. If a system or process changes, it may be that the person fears making a mistake, looking stupid or losing their perceived influence or status. Or they may be fearful of losing their job if they cannot cope with the changes.

Poor communication about the need for change and how it will impact on people can lead to them fearing the change. A way to avoid potential change pitfalls is to recognise and remember that people are different and that any change needs to be well planned and communicated in a number of ways. An important aspect of that communication is giving people plenty of confidential and supportive opportunities to ask questions and raise concerns.

The word 'change' implies a conscious approach to making a defined move from one static state to another. Of course there will be occasions where a review identifies the need for a significant and proactive change programme that does just this. However, there will be many more instances where the change is more of a 'tweak', made in response to an issue or situation. In our work or home lives and in the wider world, nothing remains completely static. People Management includes being aware of and prepared for constant evolution as well as planned change.

4. People have lives outside of work

You and your team have lives outside of work that at some point will impact upon it.

We often talk about finding a 'work life balance'. This creates the image that we have two buckets, one marked work and one marked life, balanced at each end of a see-saw. The impression is that we can divide what we do between the two buckets to keep the see-saw balanced. In reality we can't split ourselves in two; we only have one bucket. There may be a point in our lives when turmoil leads to that bucket being close to or actually falling over.

If you are a business owner or a manager then your main priority is likely to be your own organisation. The people you employ are unlikely to feel the same way, but that is not wrong and nor should you be upset or offended by this. Ultimately, when faced with a difficult situation in life, people will, quite understandably, be loyal to themselves and their families first.

The challenge in a difficult situation is to be supportive to one person, whilst managing the impact of their issues on the other people in the team who you are also responsible for supporting.

As an employer you will have a statutory responsibility as set by employment laws, for some aspects outside of work that impact on your employees' lives. This will include paying statutory sick pay and allowing unpaid time off for an emergency involving a dependent. However, this does not mean you have to be responsible for everything that happens in your employee's lives.

You are not your employee's 'nanny'. People Management is not about being responsible for managing employee's social and home lives for them or resolving any of their personal problems.

I believe that People Management includes building an open and supportive working environment as this will have positive motivational effects on a whole team. This needs to be tempered with guidelines on where an employer's responsibility starts and ends. However, issues are not always clear-cut, particularly when they involve the health of the employee or a family member. The challenge is then balancing their needs with that of your organisation during a difficult and emotional time.

From a People Management perspective being objective, ethical, open, fair and compassionate and building good lines of communication between the individual and the whole team, will help when facing difficult decisions.

5. Prepare to be unpopular

Another phrase that often springs to mind when dealing with people is that 'you can't please all of the people all of the time'. As a manager you can try to do this (and I don't know of anyone who has managed a team who deliberately wants to be unpopular) by aspiring to be a good boss who avoids the mistakes you have seen poor managers make. Even so, you can't always accurately predict how others will react to your decisions and judge your performance as a boss.

You are also likely to find yourself having to deal with matters that are not due to something that you have or haven't done. This can include mediating in personal disputes, making decisions involving disciplinary and grievance issues, or telling someone their job is redundant.

An inevitable aspect of People Management is that at some point you are likely to have to tackle unacceptable performance or behaviour, or tell someone in your team something they don't want to hear. Many people start a business or take on a managerial job not realising that they will have to give people difficult news or even dismiss someone, but it is a possibility. Whilst it is a small proportion of what you may need to do, it can have a significant emotional and long-term impact.

When dealing with a difficult issue, taking an objective, ethical, open, fair and compassionate approach to a problem will help to ensure it is handled as justly, practically and sensitively as possible. This approach can also be applied in deciding whether to terminate someone's employment and examining whether, in all conscience, it is the right thing to do. When considering such action, protecting the performance, safety and integrity of the rest of the team and the whole organisation has to be a primary consideration.

I have yet to encounter a boss who has not at some point had to deal with a difficult issue. The best managers and bosses that I have worked for or with, have recognised and promptly dealt with difficult decisions and have done so with a sense of conscience, justice, respect and empathy. They have not shirked their responsibility to make carefully considered but ultimately difficult decisions for the overall benefit of the team or the long-term benefit of an organisation.

6. We want to be like...

I have had many meetings with clients who have read about a process or approach to People Management and want to do the same thing in their team. Aspiring to improve any aspect of People Management is commendable but I would like to issue a word of warning at this point. 'Beware the case study' and doing something because someone else is doing it, or wanting to do it in exactly the same way as they are.

You may read about an organisation that is similar to yours in respect of market and employee numbers. However, your organisation will be different if only because you employ different people and you are a different type of manager.

Case studies don't give you the perfect answer for your situation, but they can give you ideas and pointers to the best approach for your People Management.

If you want to consider various ways to be a good employer and you want to see good examples, I recommend that you go to the Great Place to Work Institute's web site at www.GreatPlaceToWork.co.uk. The Institute has information and reports on the reasons why organisations are regularly voted as being the best places to work, which may be of interest to you.

If you do want to implement something new in your organisation then don't forget that 'one size does not fit all' and take the time to carefully analyse if it will work for your team and organisation.

7. It's the people, stupid...

During Bill Clinton's successful election campaign in 1992, a strategist called James Carville hung a sign up that listed three areas to focus on and one of these was "The economy, stupid." This was intended to be for internal use only but was quickly seized on, becoming a mantra that can now be applied to many situations.

If you want to know how to make any organisation of any size successful, "it's the people, stupid".

The website of the Great Place to Work Institute mentioned in the previous section contains information on a number of successful organisations. Themes common to all of them are that they focus on their people and try to ensure they:

- **Feel trusted to do their jobs.**
- **Have trust in the people they work for and with.**
- **Feel pride in what they do and enjoy doing it.**
- **Feel valued, productive and listened to.**
- **Feel supported at work when home issues impact on their work.**

This book will cover the fundamentals of People Management that will help you achieve a similar people approach in your organisation, ensuring that its focus is on 'The people, stupid'.

KEY LEADERSHIP TRAITS

As well as having a strategy that covers the fundamentals of People Management and acknowledges the seven essentials set out above, successful managers exhibit particular key leadership traits.

Successful managers readily acknowledge that the success of their organisation is down to the people they employ and have a People Plan that is an integral part of their Business Plan. The plan is not just about how many people they will need and how much they are going to cost. It includes an approach to finding, developing and supporting people who will be fundamental to the growth and development of their organisation.

They also have good self-awareness in that they recognise and have evaluated their own personality traits and leadership style. They have acknowledged that they are not qualified, experienced or expert in all of the areas of running an organisation and building a team, and so bring in people who can help, including People Management specialists.

Successful managers also demonstrate and follow the values of being objective, ethical, open, fair and compassionate and recognise the value to an organisation of the people it employs. They are prepared to make balanced decisions about tough choices and have the humility to admit mistakes if the benefit of hindsight shows they didn't get something completely right.

There is no magic wand or quick fix to being a successful leader or manager, just as there is no scientific formula for effective People Management. As with most subjects we learn, it is about reading, learning, practicing and determining what works best in a range of situations. It's not about mastering the 'art of war', or blaming someone else for 'moving your cheese'; it is about being enthusiastic, open, empathetic, engaging, empowering as well as listening and learning.

THE FIVE KEY FACTORS – PEOPLE MANAGEMENT

I have worked with good and not so good managers and have learned a lot from both. As a result I have identified Five Key Factors I believe are fundamental to managing and developing successful teams and organisations. Great leaders develop effective People Management strategies that encompass the following:

1. Enthusiasm

Successful managers and teams have a collective sense of purpose and enthusiasm about what they are doing. This is not about whooping and clapping everything. It is about having a strong belief and determination in a product, cause or service.

2. Open Communication

Successful managers openly share information where possible. It is not about being gregarious or trying to be everyone's friend. It is about fostering an environment of honest two-way communication.

3. A Head for Business and a Heart for People

Successful managers balance a head for their business and a heart for their people. They build fun working environments based on ethics, trust and open communication but remain focussed on achieving targets. They balance compassion with objectivity in tackling problems and make difficult decisions when necessary.

4. Engaging and Empowering

Successful managers embrace every opportunity to identify and use their employees' skills and experience. They enable personal development for all, including themselves. They listen, delegate appropriately and empower team members to get on with their jobs.

5. Listening and Learning

Open communication only works when you listen, learn and act. Successful managers set and follow plans but don't slavishly stick to them just to save face. They listen to feedback, admit when they are wrong and are prepared to learn from their mistakes and adapt.

SUMMARY – PEOPLE MANAGEMENT

When developing or reviewing your approach to managing people and your People Management strategy remember:

1. **People are unique, unpredictable and will not think and feel the same way as you do.**

2. **Don't just follow the crowd. Your People Management strategy and plans need to be developed to fit your organisation. Work out what is best for your organisation and the people in it and keep up to date with the subject of People Management.**

3. **The world and people's lives (including your own) don't stand still; embrace and capitalise on constant evolution and change.**

4. **Organisations are only as successful as the people in them and effective leaders influence that success. Effective leaders have self-awareness of the impact they have on their team and take an objective, ethical, open, fair and compassionate approach to People Management and to making difficult decisions.**

5. **As the boss, make sure you apply the Five Key Factors in your approach to People Management.**

In the next chapter we'll look at the 'Boss Effect' and the impact that your personality, approach and behaviour can have on the management of your team.

CHAPTER TWO

THE BOSS EFFECT

If at some stage in your working life you are put in charge of people, you become the boss. It may be by choice or accident, and you may be in charge of one or hundreds.

Being the boss means that as well as doing your own work, you will have people looking to you for guidance and support with theirs. They will look for you to lead by example, blame you for things that go wrong and may not give you credit when things go right!

A look online for definitions of 'boss' will throw up hundreds of words and phrases. My favourites include 'big cheese', 'standard bearer' and 'top dog'. However, I have worked with many different managers and I have come to realise that there is no set specification that defines the perfect boss.

Being the boss, and the type of boss you are, will impact on your team. As a result you need to consider what is involved in being a boss and the influence of your own boss effect on team members.

A GOOD PLACE TO START: IT'S ALL ABOUT YOU

In all likelihood you are the boss because you have the drive and technical skills to set up a business, or to impress others enough to be put in charge of part of theirs. It might not be uppermost in your mind, but when you become a boss it is a good time to conduct an honest assessment of your management skills. Doing so will reap future benefits, particularly as more emphasis is placed on your management responsibilities rather than the technical work you previously focused on.

When you take on the management of people be prepared to take on other non-work issues that come with them. As well as dealing with the responsibility and challenges of recruiting, training and developing people, you may have to manage external factors that impact on their working life such as illness, family problems and household disasters. This means that your working day will include the management of others as well as the work that you are good at.

At some point you may find yourself with the dilemma that managing people takes you away from the work you enjoy doing – the reason you were promoted, or started your own business.

The natural progression of a successful organisation or team is expansion and an increase in employee numbers. For a small organisation this may mean bringing in people to do particular tasks, such as administration and accounts. If the growth is more substantive you may need to recruit people to do the technical work you do, and in time their expertise could exceed yours. Are you prepared for the point at which the people you employ overtake you in respect of their technical skills and competence?

THE PARETO PRINCIPLE

As a boss you need to consider how your own day-to-day tasks will change and how much you are involved in the daily activities and lives of your team.

You may find in time that the Pareto Principle applies to your working day. The Pareto principle (also known as the 80:20 rule) states that, for many events, roughly 80% of the effects come from 20% of the causes. Joseph M Juran (1975), a pioneer in the development of the principles and methods for managing quality control programmes, gave the name "Pareto" to the principle of the "vital few and trivial many" after Italian economist, Vilfredo Pareto. Pareto observed in 1906 that 80% of the land in Italy was owned by 20% of the population. You may find that 80% of your day will be spent on managing people and their tasks, and 20% will be spent on managing yourself and your own tasks.

Will you see it as positive or negative that you are not needed for the day-to-day technical work that you're really good at? Don't feel threatened by this; instead you should congratulate yourself on your success in recruiting and developing people who can get on with the work without you. This will enable you to focus on what you need to do to develop yourself and the success of your organisation.

You will need to think about how you are going to adjust to this personally, and how you are going to adjust your organisation so it is not negatively impacted. It can be time consuming, stressful and could damage your organisation if you carry on trying to do everything that you were doing as well as managing other people.

As the person responsible for the People Management of individuals or teams then you need to be aware of what I call the 'Boss Effect'.

WHAT'S YOUR 'BOSS EFFECT'?

If you want your business or department to do more than survive but also to thrive, you need to think about how your Boss Effect will impact on everyone.

Investing the effort in working out your boss style can save you time and money and help you to manage more confidently and competently. One of the most obvious and useful development opportunities is to learn from the good habits of successful bosses and the bad habits from others.

The main trap to avoid is trying to be something you are not. It is unlikely to work and will make for an unpleasant experience for you and your employees. The more you understand about yourself as a manager, the more these skills are going to prove useful in managing others.

If you haven't already done so, consider investing in training designed to help you to identify your leadership and management style.

As part of considering your style of leadership and management, ask yourself the following questions:

1. ***What are your work values and how do they translate into your work behaviours?***

   For example, do you want your employees to feel valued, supported and included at work? Or are you not really bothered about how they feel, as they are only there to do a job?

2. ***What is your approach to life?***

   Are you a 'work hard; play hard' or 'it can wait until tomorrow' kind of person? How will that translate into the working environment of your organisation? What employment experience do you want for you and your employees?

3. ***Why are you doing what you are doing?***

   If you are in a particular job, or have set up a business, even if you didn't start out intending to employ people, what keeps you doing it? The reasons may range from self-preservation because you need to work to pay the bills, to being self-employed because you are not good at being employed by someone else. If your answer to this question is that you are a reluctant boss and have found yourself doing by it accident rather than design, then an additional question for you is "Do you really want to be a boss?" If the answer is no, I suggest you consider a change of role that doesn't require you to manage others. Focus on work you enjoy doing, rather than risk becoming a bad boss.

Working out the answers to these three questions will help you with many aspects of People Management including recruitment, reward, training, development and team motivation.

A BOSS WITH PERSONALITY

As you will read in Chapter 3, it is my experience that successful People Management is a mix of science, art and luck. For the science aspect of being a boss, training that includes personality profiling can help you to understand your individual personality. Your personality will shape your behaviours that impact on your leadership style and influence the type of boss you are.

There is no perfect template of personality, just as there is no perfect template for the best way to lead and manage. Everyone is different and we all have strengths and weaknesses. Whilst you may wish to have a different personality, the reality is that your basic character cannot fundamentally change. However, you can develop aspects of your personality that you are less happy with by consciously working on your behaviour.

If you are a shy introvert, you are not going to change your core personality to become an extravert. What you can do is work on your confidence with training and practice. Then, when you next have to go into a room full of people you have never met before, rather than standing quietly not speaking to anyone, you can make use of tips you have learned on how to behave differently by initiating conversations.

Personality should not be used to excuse behaviours that are unacceptable. An awareness of your personality can help you develop positive behaviours that will help you lead and manage others. You will also be better placed to challenge the unacceptable behaviours of others.

The art of being a boss is about becoming skilled through practice but it is highly likely that practice will lead to mistakes as well as successes. As with developing any new skill, self appraisal after good and bad experiences will help you to learn from both. You also need to acknowledge that you will never stop learning.

Luck may also play a part. There will be occasions where an experience, good or bad, is due more to chance than what you have consciously done or said. As mentioned in Chapter 3, the likelihood is that the more practice you put into the art of being the boss, the luckier you will become.

LONELY AT THE TOP

As the boss, you may find yourself on a path of promotion that takes you up the corporate ladder. You may also find that whilst you have more people reporting to you, there are fewer or even no people above you; as the adage says it can be tough at the top.

One thing you can do in this situation is to find yourself an experienced and trusted mentor. This is someone you can turn to for help and advice or to share ideas about your team and organisation.

Even the most successful leaders had to start somewhere. Many are willing to act as a mentor and share their experiences, from the mistakes they made to what they did that was successful. They can question and test your ideas and be a good source of contacts and advice.

One client I work with has built mentoring into the personal development plan for everyone in the organisation. All their employees, whatever their level of experience or seniority, are helped to identify and approach a mentor if they want one. They can use work time to meet with their mentor. There are no rules other than that the relationship is private and confidential. Employees are asked if they have a mentor to measure the take up of the scheme, but they do not have to say who it is or what they talk about, unless they want to.

Comments from the employees who take up the opportunity include that this 'no strings attached' approach makes them feel valued, and that the organisation is genuinely interested in their personal development. Many find it easier to talk to their mentor than their line manager about a difficult work issue, and their mentor has helped them to resolve the problem.

This scheme has a major pay back to the organisation in that employees report that they are more motivated and less likely to leave. The organisation has shown that encouraging people to have mentors can lead to improved productivity, saving money on employee turnover and effectively resolving work problems.

You may be the boss but you are an employee too, so the benefits will be the same for you. If you have worked with a great boss or have heard of someone through other sources, then why not approach them to be your mentor?

But remember, good advice doesn't just come from a mentor; it can also come from members of your team.

TALK TO ME

Being a boss will require you to communicate regularly with your team.

As set out in Chapter 1, a key factor I have seen demonstrated by effective bosses is open communication. A good way to facilitate open communication is to have regular one to one meetings with every member of your team (not just the most vocal or overtly ambitious!).

The meetings can provide you with data and a forum for two-way feedback that can contribute to the development of individuals, teams and the whole organisation. They are an opportunity to ask People Management 'health check' questions to evaluate; organisation and personal performance, work progress, targets, objectives, deadlines, and opportunities for personal development.

The meeting is not just a forum for you to talk at people, it is also an opportunity for you to listen. A meeting is more effective if it is a shared, open and collaborative conversation where what can be achieved together is discussed and agreed.

Regularly scheduling but then cancelling or truncating meetings, will be counterproductive. Not only is it bad manners, it creates the impression that your time is more valuable than others. Team members will give up preparing for and participating in the meetings if you don't show respect for their importance.

If you are already having meetings, check if they are effective and efficient. Be honest in your assessment of your performance and ask for feedback from your team.

I am not advocating you spend all day in meetings or that you ask the same questions in the same order at every meeting. It is up to you to find the balance that works for you and each team member.

A culture of constructive criticism and feedback can be developed by asking your team for their questions, input and feedback. Employees need to be reassured that raising a problem or concern is not rude, disloyal or means they are a 'snitch'. As a Boss you need to demonstrate that speaking up and giving constructive feedback as a 'critical friend' can lead to changes and improvements. It particularly includes how you behave if people are critical of what you are doing or proposing. Becoming defensive, over protective or bristling with obvious annoyance is not helpful and will put people off from being open and honest.

One thing to avoid at the meetings is just focussing on problems. Don't forget that feedback also includes what is going well. Positives are just as useful as negatives and all information is pertinent to help develop individuals, teams and organisations.

As the Boss you need to be conscious that people do not automatically think that what you suggest is what you want to happen. See the 'Impact of Your Boss Effect' section of this chapter. An aspect of one to one meetings is to ensure that people see your suggestions or comments as just that, and they are not interpreted as interference or an edict.

A vital aspect of meetings is to agree the follow up actions. This includes what is or isn't shared with others outside of the meeting, particularly with what could be sensitive personal information. It is particularly important that you do what you say you will do, or keep people informed why if that is not possible. Having regular meetings doesn't mean that you don't communicate at other times!

IMPACT OF YOUR 'BOSS EFFECT'

The impact of your 'Boss Effect' covers pretty much everything you say and everything you do. You may be frustrated at the impact your employees are having on you, but have you stopped to think about the impact you are having on them? From your style of verbal and written communication through to your body language, be aware that however benign the comment, email or frown, people can and will take it personally.

Be aware that in many cases, people will take what you say as being what needs to be done, because you are the boss. Whilst you may say, "Have you thought about doing it this way?" to offer an alternative to consider, an employee may interpret that as being 'the boss has said that we have to do it this way'.

Also, the approach to work that you demonstrate and the hours that you put in will set the style and tone for your team. If you want to run yourself into the ground then that is your choice. But it is not good practice, good business, ethical or lawful to run your team into the ground too.

When bosses working this way are questioned, they usually tell me that they don't ask people to follow the same approach they are taking. The counter argument is that unless clearly told otherwise, employees will interpret your behaviours and what you say as being what you expect from them.

THE FRIENDLY BOSS

Remember that we all have different personalities which impacts on our behaviour, so think carefully about your personality and how your behaviour impacts on others. This is particularly true in situations where the boss is a friend or relative of the people that they manage.

I have often been called in to help with problems when an employee has been promoted to become the boss of a team where they were previously a peer and a friend of people within it. The problems are usually linked to issues of friends becoming foes. I have also helped to resolve similar problems where people who are already the boss, recruit and have to manage family or friends.

However much you think it won't happen (or you try not to let it), promotion and being the boss does change the dynamic between you, family, friends or people you have previously worked alongside. It doesn't mean that you can't make it work. The transition can be made easier by taking a pragmatic and proactive approach and planning for the effects of this change. This includes talking openly and honestly to people and asking for their thoughts about how things may be different. Acknowledging potential pitfalls and agreeing boundaries can prevent difficult situations or help tackle them if they do arise.

It is possible to remain friends with your employees or direct reports, but you have to remember that as the boss, you may have to make difficult decisions or take actions that could upset them. How will you feel if you need to tackle family or friends about their poor attendance or performance, or if you have to tell them their job is redundant?

Socialising and getting to know your employees is good for building positive interpersonal relationships and teamwork. However, remember the boundaries and keep an eye on your own behaviour. This may seem obvious as you read it but I know of many a boss or HR manager who has had to deal with the fallout from a party or event. If this leads to a grievance or disciplinary matter, make sure you are the one doing the judging and are not the one being judged!

This applies whether you are at 'official' work events, or if you are socialising outside normal working hours. I have seen many situations where a boss has tried to be 'one of the gang' and an indiscreet word or action has backfired. If you are a boss then to your employees you are a boss 24/7.

THE FIVE KEY FACTORS – THE BOSS EFFECT

The Five Key Factors embodied by good managers I first described in Chapter 1 can be applied to your approach to being a boss:

1. Enthusiasm

A good boss requires drive. Take responsibility for leading the team during both the good and the difficult times.

2. Open Communication

Make yourself available to all employees and regularly communicate what is happening within the organisation. Successful bosses recognise the advantages of having and encouraging an open and collaborative approach. They listen, share, agree and act.

3. A Head for Business and a Heart for People

Good bosses do more than the minimum; they have a genuine desire to do right by their employees. They develop a friendly, collaborative working environment, whilst maintaining clear boundaries and standards of behaviour. They encourage fun, but regulate performance and make difficult decisions when necessary. Successful bosses are objective, fair, ethical, open, and compassionate, but they are not pushovers.

4. Engaging and Empowering

Successful bosses develop teams that can operate without them. They maximise performance by engaging and empowering all employees. This enables them to focus on essential strategic planning for the long term benefit of the organisation. They don't interfere with the minutiae of everyday operation, but monitor the overall picture and act where necessary.

5. Listening and Learning

Good bosses will learn about and understand their leadership skills, and thereby adapt their behaviour to get the best from their team. They recognise the benefit of guidance from a coach or mentor and they learn from their failures and successes.

SUMMARY – THE BOSS EFFECT

Being aware of all aspects of being a boss and your 'Boss Effect' can make life easier and more enjoyable for everyone. The Boss Effect is not just about being a nice boss; it is about doing the right thing in the right way and at the right time, for you and your team. The hard-nosed business case is that it can improve productivity, and is a significant factor that will impact on the success of your organisation.

Whether you are a new or an experienced boss then as well as adhering to the Five Key Factors, it is prudent to remember:

1. **Be prepared to do more People Management and less of the things you have been doing.**

2. **Learning about People Management, leadership, management styles and understanding more about your own approach will help you and your team.**

3. **Have fun and build an open and collaborative working environment, but be prepared to make and implement difficult decisions that will impact negatively on people you like.**

4. **Be prepared to employ and develop people who will know more about a subject than you do.**

5. **As the boss, look to apply the five key factors and remember the impact that what you do and what you say can have – don't underestimate your Boss Effect.**

In Chapter 3 we'll discuss how People Management is a combination of science, art and luck and how an awareness and understanding of the potential of all three can help you to effectively manage the individuals in your team.

CHAPTER THREE

SCIENCE, ART OR LUCK?

If asked whether People Management is about science, art or luck, my answer would be that it is a combination of all three. In different situations the mix and proportions vary but they all play their part in some way.

As you read this book you will see that there are no ready-made or rigid People Management processes. If I put the science, art or luck question to successful entrepreneurs such as Sir Richard Branson or Lord Sugar, their answers would doubtless be significantly different. But one thing that is common to them, and to every other entrepreneur, is acknowledging they wouldn't be successful without people.

People recognise that they need to study, learn and continually practice the principles of a particular skill, such as computer coding, finance or engineering. Many of them will be responsible not only for their area of skill or competence, but also for People Management. However, very few will study, learn or continually practice the principles of People Management. They often assume that they inherently know, or have an instinct for the subject. Others haven't considered that it is a subject matter in its own right that has years of learning and research behind it.

As a manager, the science of People Management involves the practical application of learning gained from research into the behaviour of individuals and groups.

As I said in the introduction to this book, it is not a textbook and it would be impossible to attempt to cover in detail the vast amounts of research and thinking relating to People Management. There are many excellent sources of information available online and in libraries and I advocate that managers are proactive in learning about the tricky subject of people. To get you started, I am going to cover the main elements of science, art and luck that I have found useful to understand with respect to People Management.

A GOOD PLACE TO START: A SCIENTIFIC SUMMARY

As a starting point I have summarised below the areas of science that I have found useful for People Management.

Behavioural science, which includes the study of people and People Management, can trace its roots back to the early 20th century. A set of experiments conducted by an Australian born sociologist called Elton Mayo (1933) has become one of the most famous pieces of research.

The experiments that took place in the 1930s were designed to look at how productivity might be affected by physical conditions in a factory. The factory was the Western Electric factory in Hawthorne; a suburb of Chicago. The location gave its name to what is now called the 'Hawthorne Effect'.

Mayo's experiments looked at two groups of workers in the factory. For one group the lighting was improved whilst for the control group the lighting stayed the same. Results showed greater productivity for the improved lighting group compared to the control group. Further experiments involved changing other conditions, such as working hours. After each change it was found that productivity increased further.

However, it was subsequently found that even when the lighting was reverted to the original level, productivity continued to improve. In fact, the research showed that even when everything in the factory was changed back to how it was before the experiments started, absenteeism had dropped and productivity was at its highest level. Hence, making changes to the physical working environment wasn't the only reason for the increase in productivity.

The conclusion from the experiments was that productivity was improved because of the interest that had been taken in the employees. It showed that all it took to increase productivity was for someone to be concerned about the employees and their workplace, and to give them the opportunity to discuss any changes before they took place.

Another area of People Management science that you are likely to find yourself talking about in relation to your employees is personality. I am sure that at some point you have used the phrase 'a personality clash'. The field of personality research is vast and covers many areas, from psychology, to the molecular genetics of the brain. The earliest thinking into personality can be traced back to 300 years BC to Plato and Aristotle! Much of the more recent research into personality has tried to classify a set of identifiable personality factors common to all of us, such as emotional stability and sensitivity. It has also looked at how these common factors may influence us in respect of how we feel and think, what we want and what we do.

The number of research papers and books written on this subject is enormous. However, a common feature of much of this research is that, despite identifying a number of common personality traits or factors, everyone is unique. That is why when looking to fill a vacancy saying "I need to recruit another me" will not work. There isn't another you!

There is no right or wrong personality, nor is there a template that will tell you what personality factors make up the perfect employee. You may employ two equally skilled people; one may be outgoing and friendly, the other introverted and morose. If they are both working well and are producing a high quantity and quality of work, then they are equally valuable to your organisation.

I have learnt from the science of personality that having an awareness of the subject is not a guarantee of becoming an infallible judge of people and how they will behave.

In Chapter 1 I talked about how the only predictable thing about people is that they are unpredictable. This is borne out by the work of an eminent psychotherapist, Dr. Albert Ellis who said:

> *"…humans are born with a strong tendency: one, to think about their thinking, to reason, to actualise themselves, to live and sustain themselves happily; and two, unfortunately, a tendency to foolishly, irrationally defeat themselves and their social groups".*
> Albert Ellis (1984).

Ellis observed early in his career that a key component of human personality is irrationality, which often leads to cognitive, emotional and behavioural dysfunction. He asserted that people are naturally irrational and prefer short-term satisfaction of wants rather than longer term benefits. That is why it is impossible to predict with 100% accuracy what someone may do, or how they may behave in a given situation.

Reading and learning about personality has also helped me to realise that there is no formula to follow that will tell you exactly what mix of personality traits will create perfect performance or the best leaders.

The science of personality demonstrates that effective People Management requires an awareness of your own personality as well as considering a variety of approaches to suit the personalities of other people.

The result of the Hawthorne Effect has reinforced what I have seen in practice, namely that engaging with employees can positively influence their performance. It is not about standing over them, watching and dictating everything that they do. It is about involving people in decisions affecting them and being interested in them, their surroundings and the people they are working with.

IS INTELLIGENCE ENOUGH?

Another area of research linked to people that has implications for People Management is intelligence. Research includes experiments that look to measure and quantify intelligence, whilst others examine the impact of intelligence on successful leadership. A common misconception is that intelligence is an accurate indicator of leadership ability.

In their book 'Organisations and the Psychological Contract: Managing People at Work', Peter Makin et al (1996) state:

> "Many personality traits have been examined, but few show any relationship to successful leadership. One possible exception is 'intelligence' which is not, however, a personality trait, but an aptitude. According to some early researchers (e.g. Stogdill, 1948) there is some relationship, although it would appear to be curvilinear, rather than a straight-line relationship. In other words, while leadership ability increases with increasing intelligence, it does so only up to a certain point. Beyond this point higher levels of intelligence lead to decreased leadership ability".
> (Makin, P., et al. 1996, p.174-175).

This means that the cleverest person in a team is not automatically the best person to be in charge of it. In my experience this is also often the case when applied to the most technically competent or the most experienced person in a team. Whilst that person can demonstrate a high level of work aptitude, it is not a given that they will be an effective team leader.

I have seen many cases where someone has been promoted to lead a team because they are the longest serving employee, or they are the most skilled at a technical job. Often there was no interview process and if there was, it did not include an assessment of the person's ability to lead and motivate others, or to deal with difficult people issues. In addition they had not been prepared for managing people and for having less time to do the job that they were previously doing. The collective negative consequence of this was a stressed manager, a disaffected team and a drop in productivity. The learning from the science here is to have a process in place that ensures that you are appointing the person most suited to a role and not just the longest serving, the most skilled or the most intelligent.

The science of intelligence has expanded beyond just measuring a person's intelligence quotient (IQ) and now includes other parallel considerations such as emotional intelligence (EQ). This thinking came to the fore in the 1990s, when a science reporter at The New York Times called Daniel Goleman came across an article in a small academic journal by two psychologists, John Mayer and Peter Salovey (1990) who proposed a concept they called 'Emotional Intelligence'.

Goleman went on to write a hugely successful book on the subject called 'Emotional Intelligence: Why it can matter more than IQ' (2006). Emotional intelligence is seen as the way we manage emotions, both our own and those of others. Goleman argues that emotional intelligence plays a crucial role in determining happiness and success via how we control our impulses, self-motivation, empathy and social competence in our relationships with others.

On his website (www.danielgoleman.info), Goleman states; "Now I see that social intelligence – empathy and social skill – are essentials for effective leadership, although very often people are promoted to leadership positions because they have gotten excellent results as a sole performer. But if they lack social intelligence they will flounder."

The argument is that at work and in life, whilst intelligence and work ethic are important, they are not the only factors that influence success or failure. Advocates contend that research shows that EQ demonstrated through empathy and social skills is essential to effective leadership.

I have learned that IQ, or exceptional technical skills and competence, are not in themselves accurate indicators of effective performance or leadership. What also needs to be considered is a candidate's EQ in respect of their skills to empathise and build effective relationships with others.

WHAT ABOUT ART AND LUCK?

Learning about the science of people is only one part of the People Management puzzle; another piece involves the art of applying that learning. One dictionary definition of art defines it as a skill that is typically acquired through practice. The art of People Management involves taking the science and applying it through the application of judgement and common sense to put it into practice in the day-to-day management of people.

The art of People Management includes realising that the slavish application of science to all situations and to all people in exactly the same way each time is unlikely to lead to success.

Science shows that people are different. This thinking needs to be applied even when you find yourself in a situation that appears identical to one previously encountered, such as managing poor performance. Whilst your approach may be similar in setting and monitoring targets, the art is in tailoring the details of the conversations and support to suit the individual.

Not everyone gets it right all of the time, but good leaders demonstrate the art of learning from their mistakes in order to do it better next time. One of the most well known and often quoted leaders is Winston Churchill. He attributed much of his later success to lessons learned from mistakes made in his early political career. There is often more to be learnt from mistakes than from successes.

The last piece of the puzzle is luck. Many entrepreneurs have stories about how a defining success or failure came about through chance, rather than something they had consciously done. My observation on luck is that you need to influence it as much as you can by taking conscious action. This can include avoiding circumstances that will hinder you and putting yourself into situations that can help. An example of this with People Management is with recruitment. You can make conscious decisions about a role, how it is described and where it is advertised. These actions can influence your success in appointing a good candidate who may come across your advert by chance.

There is a famous and often used saying about luck that is a favourite of mine. Variations of it are attributed to different people but the quote that sticks in my mind is the one that is credited to the very successful golfer Gary Player. Someone had suggested he had been lucky with some of his golf shots. He replied by saying "The harder I practice, the luckier I get."

One of the actions you can take in respect of influencing your luck in People Management is to learn more about the subject and to put that learning into practice.

THE FIVE KEY FACTORS – SCIENCE, ART OR LUCK?

The Five Key Factors embodied by managers I first described in Chapter 1 can be applied to your approach to the science, art and luck of People Management:

1. Enthusiasm

Successful leaders are eager to learn and to keep learning. They are keen to evaluate and try new approaches and to learn from their mistakes as well as their successes.

2. Open Communication

Be open in sharing thoughts and ideas about new science, ideas and thinking with your teams. It also includes being open about admitting when a mistake has been made or something has gone wrong, so that lessons can be learned.

3. A Head for Business and a Heart for People

Understanding and practicing the science and art of People Management will lead to increased productivity and engaged employees. Engaged employees are likely to be happier and more settled in their roles.

4. Engaging and Empowering

Successful leaders recognise that this approach is good for business. Remember that the conclusions from the science of the Hawthorne experiments showed that increased productivity was due to taking an interest in and involving employees.

5. Listening and Learning

Listen when people share an idea or express concern over your ideas. Learn from those same people and from the science, the art and the luck of People Management!

SUMMARY – SCIENCE, ART OR LUCK?

Successful People Management is a combination of many elements that come together to influence positive outcomes. Science and the art of learning from it, by putting it into practice, will enable you to maximise opportunities to influence your luck in being a successful manager.

At any stage of your experience of People Management keep in mind that:

1. To influence your luck, you need to take opportunities to put into practice what has been learned from the science of People Management.

2. There is no fixed approach to People Management or ideal template of personality.

3. Success in any role is not just about intelligence as defined by a person's IQ; emotional intelligence is a contributing factor.

4. Effective leaders keep learning from improvements in science and from their successes and failures.

5. Follow the five key factors of science, art and luck to ensure that what you learn, understand and experience is translated into actions that build an effective team.

In the next chapter I describe three theories that can help you to make sense of the challenges of People Management not just with individuals but also with teams and the whole organisation.

CHAPTER FOUR

THREE THEORIES THAT MAKE SENSE

In Chapter 3 I discuss the science, art and luck of People Management and focus on these elements as applied to individuals. However, the overall success of an organisation is not just down to individuals. It is also dependent on how they function in teams, and how those teams operate within the whole organisation. In this chapter I am going to look at three theories that encompass individuals, teams and the whole organisation, which can help you to make sense of People Management.

A recent online search for the phrase 'people management theories' yielded a result listing over 700 books. Many of them contain theories developed by academics from scientific studies and research. Others advocate ideas and credos about People Management by commentators ranging from Winnie the Pooh to an ancient military strategist called Sun Tzu.

I encourage any manager to read and learn about different People Management theories, but with a myriad of information available this chapter will look at three that I have found useful.

During my time in People Management I have encountered many theories and studies. Whilst I can't say that any one in particular has proved revolutionary, some have challenged my thinking, broadened my understanding and provided me with a source of useful tools. In particular I have found the theories outlined in this chapter useful in shaping my thinking about People Management and why people do what they do. They provide a greater understanding of the effective management of people and can help you avoid pitfalls that impede your organisation. You can also use them as a place to start analysing issues when they arise. The three theories are underpinned by the concept of the 'psychological contract' that exists between an employer and an employee.

Psychologists define the psychological contract as exchanges that take place that impact on and influence how we think, feel and behave.

Contracts, whether psychological or financial, involve an exchange. We regularly enter into financial contacts that involve the exchange of money for goods or services, from the formal signing of a mobile phone contract, to the informal paying of cash for a lunchtime sandwich. There is an implicit financial contract if you are paid in exchange for carrying out an agreed type and amount of work.

In the work environment just as important as the financial contract are the implicit expectations of the psychological contract. As an employee it is not unreasonable to expect that as well as pay, our employer provides work in a safe environment, free from harm and distress.

The difference between how people expect to be treated and how they are treated can have an impact on how they work, and therefore, how you manage them. An eminent psychologist, Edgar Schein (1980), said "Though it remains unwritten, the Psychological Contract is a powerful determiner of behaviour."

Expectations that are not met by an employer can lead to feelings of disappointment and mistrust, and can result in an employee rethinking their relationship with the organisation. Behaviour linked to broken expectations can range from an individual sulking, to the whole organisation taking industrial action and walking out.

Regardless of the level of behaviour, the outcome is the same; a breach of the psychological contract has a negative impact on performance and productivity.

A GOOD PLACE TO START: THREE THEORIES THAT MAKE SENSE

The following three theories will help you to develop a better understanding of what lies behind the psychological contract that a manger has with employees. This in turn can help you to make sense of the motivations and behaviours of individuals and teams and how these can be used to build a high performing team.

Theory One – Maslow's Hierarchy of Needs

This theory can help us to understand the needs that employees expect their employers to fill as part of the psychological contract.

If you ask your employees to list out the reasons why they need to work, their answers are likely to be different, as will the motivations behind their reasons for doing the type of work that they do.

The history of research into motivation stretches back to 1911, and beyond, but one of the first comprehensive attempts to classify it into various needs was undertaken by Abraham Maslow in the 1940s. Maslow's theory, that needs can be categorised and classified as a hierarchy, is usually depicted as a pyramid as shown on page 48.

Maslow suggested five major need categories. He starts with basic physiological needs and moves up through a hierarchy of security, social and esteem needs, to the need that he called self-actualisation.

Level 1 – Physiological Needs:
The need for food, drink and oxygen.

Level 2 – Security Needs:
The security of self, family and property.

Level 3 – Social Needs:
Acceptance and affection, friendship and belonging to a group.

Level 4 – Esteem Needs:
Self-esteem, achievement, approval and respect of others.

Level 5 – Self-Actualisation:
The need to develop skills, to become what we believe we are capable of becoming, so that we are self-fulfilled.

MASLOW'S HIERARCHY OF NEEDS

Level 5
Self-actualisation
Self-fulfillment
Becoming what we believe
we are capable of becoming

Level 4
Esteem - self-esteem, confidence,
achievements, respect of others

Level 3
Social - friendship, family, acceptance,
affection, love

Level 2
Security - body, employment, family, home, health,
resources

Level 1
Physiological - breathing, water, food, sex, sleep

HOW DOES THIS HELP YOU AT WORK?

This theory helps show that as human beings we look for more than just an acceptable level of pay from employers. Successful People Managers understand that exceeding the minimum of the financial and the psychological contracts will motivate and develop a high performing team.

In a society with a welfare state, we would hope that everyone has access to ways of fulfilling the basic physiological needs of Level 1 for food, water and oxygen.

From the point of view of the work place, we can impact on Level 2 by ensuring that the security needs of employee's are met. From the aspect of the financial contract, this includes a fair level of pay for the work an employee does to provide security for themselves and their family. From the aspect of the psychological contract, security also covers providing an environment that does not damage an employee's physical or mental health. From an effective People Management perspective, security does not just mean fair pay and safe tools or methods of working. It includes not putting people under unmanageable levels of stress and making sure they are not bullied or harassed.

Maslow argued that the needs at each level have to be met before the next level becomes important. If we get the working environment right and meet an employee's Level 2 security needs and then Level 3 social needs with employees feeling accepted and supported in a friendly environment, we are more likely to have motivated employees who want to achieve. Receiving acknowledgement and approval through feedback about how they are performing and what they are achieving, will help employees meet their Level 4 self-esteem needs. As a result of these exchanges, they will be more likely to want to develop skills to improve themselves, and be self-fulfilled and achieve their Level 5 self-actualisation need. All this will ultimately benefit your organisation through increased performance.

What we have to remember is that a move up from one level to the next does not mean that we can forget about the previous one. So if pay and benefits don't remain competitive, or you don't tackle what, to you, may be a trivial issue but is an important security need to someone else, problems will arise. Needs from the financial and the psychological contract that are not met can lead to behaviour issues including absence and fallouts between team members.

This is why it is important to communicate with your employees, to find out if their work needs are being met and to invest in training which develops higher levels of achievement and job satisfaction. It will help make your job easier and your organisation more productive.

Don't assume that every employee's needs and motivations are the same. Whilst the path to self-actualisation for one employee is to climb the promotional ladder to earn a bigger salary, for another it is to have a quiet life receiving competitive pay and benefits, doing the same administrative job for 30 years.

WHY IS IT USEFUL?

Maslow's Hierarchy of Needs is a useful theory to remember when planning the basic structures to meet employee needs for pay, a safe and supportive working environment, training and development, communications and team building. It makes sound business sense to consciously plan and invest in these structures and failing to do so will cost your business.

It is also useful to remember that whilst there are five levels of needs, the actual factors within them that motivate individual employees will differ. For example, don't assume that what works in meeting the Level 3 social needs for acceptance for one employee will work for another. Effective People Management is about working out the unique needs for individuals. This includes being aware that one person will want to be sociable at work whilst another will be more withdrawn.

Since the publication of Maslow's concept of the Hierarchy of Needs, there has been criticism of its lack of scientific evidence to back up the theory. However, the basis of the theory is a simple way of representing what is a complex subject. Many psychology textbooks don't now include Maslow, but as a management theory it is still a useful way of illustrating motivations behind our behaviour.

Maslow's theory shows that whilst there are many different elements that combine to impact on motivation, there are factors common to all employees that influence a drive to ascend the hierarchy of needs.

Effective People Management includes awareness of these factors and developing ways to meet common needs, whilst also identifying individual approaches to harness different motivations.

Theory Two – Open Systems Theory

Prior to the 1960s, theories about organisations looked at how they operated as closed systems, without factoring in outside influences. In the 1960s theories emerged which recognised that external environmental influences could significantly impact on organisations and that as such they are 'open systems'.

An open system can be an organisation or a group, and can involve a process or people. It applies to organisations or groups of any size or complexity.

THE ORGANISATION AS AN OPEN MODEL

From Cummings & Worley

The 'open systems' model from Cummings and Worley (2008) shows how an organisation can operate in a way that achieves its goals. An open system such as an organisation does not operate in isolation but within an environment. This environment includes factors outside the organisation that can have a direct or indirect impact on performance and what the organisation actually achieves.

For an organisation, examples of direct environment factors include changes in employment or tax legislation, suppliers putting up their prices and competitors bringing out new products. Indirect factors can include cultural values such as the importance of being carbon neutral. They can also include the prevailing political environment, such as a desire to more closely regulate banking or to make changes to employment and pension laws.

To operate, an organisation takes inputs from the external environment. These inputs will include employees, materials and services such as electricity. The inputs are transformed using various processes involving people and systems that result in an output, which can be a product or a service. These outputs go into the external environment and feedback from their usage determines how the organisation is doing, and provides impetus for change and improvement.

An example is a baker who specialises in making fancy cup cakes. The external environment sets direct factors around health and safety law, and food hygiene rules. Indirect factors can include the trend for fancy cup cakes to replace traditional wedding cakes. The inputs include a crack team of employees who use ingredients and state of the art machinery, powered by electricity to transform those ingredients into an output of a range of cup cakes. Feedback from the sales of the cup cakes, both of the actual numbers sold and the comments gathered from customers, will influence future inputs with regard to ingredients, changes to the range, number of cup cakes baked, etc.

HOW DOES THIS HELP YOU AT WORK?

An understanding of open systems theory can help us to become more aware of the aspects of People Management that affect an organisation or a team of employees.

The theory of open systems helps us to recognise and understand that all systems are unique. For example, even though two organisations both make cup cakes, how they do it, why they do it, and the external and internal factors that impact on them will be different.

It helps us to understand that we cannot completely control organisational environment factors, but that we can manage our inputs, transformations, outputs and feedback in response to these.

WHY IS IT USEFUL?

When analysing the performance of an organisation, this theory helps us to consider all of the factors that contribute to that performance. It can also act as a tool to help you diagnose issues within your organisation to solve problems, make changes and improve effectiveness.

It establishes how the performance of an organisation and its people relies not only on internal factors, but also on the external environment. Hence change is inevitable and unavoidable. Furthermore, it shows that using the template elsewhere will not necessarily work due to the impact of different external and internal factors.

With regard to employees it is vital to have processes that encourage feedback about the inputs, processes and outputs impacting on themselves, the team and the organisation. This will help improve their individual performance as well as that of the whole organisation.

Open Systems Theory shows that as people and organisations we cannot expect to live in isolation, protected from factors outside our control and influence. It also shows that there needs to be a constant flow between what we do and what we produce. With respect to the People Management of individuals, teams and organisations, feedback is an essential part of maintaining and improving that flow.

Theory Three – Edge of Chaos

Various definitions can be found for the 'Edge of Chaos' and many of these talk about it being a point between order and randomness. For me, the following quote from Peter Senge, an American scientist, sums up what I would consider to be the Edge of Chaos when applied to People Management.

> "Organisations are dynamic systems in a continuous state of adaption and improvement."

Expecting to get to a point when things will remain static is an unrealistic ambition and can hold back the performance and success of you, your employees and your organisation. Don't fall into the trap of thinking the result of a particular action will mean all is well and you can leave a plan in place for 12 months before you take another look at the organisation.

People, customers and the external environment all conspire against stability. The only constant is that your organisation will always be in a state of flux, with no one day being the same as the next. Even if you didn't plan to be there and are not comfortable being there, you may find yourself in a situation of having to manage on the Edge of Chaos.

At this point it is worth making the distinction between managing processes and people that are changing, and being a chaotic and disorganised manager. Creating the chaos yourself will not help anyone! Disorganised chaos can cause unacceptable levels of stress that will lead to undermining the psychological contract between you and your team.

It also doesn't mean that we should seek to avoid establishing stability in respect of factors that impact on the organisation such as annual business plans, team numbers and regular processes. What it does mean is acknowledging that, whilst parameters for these can be set, they will need to flex with the changing needs of the organisation and external factors.

As people managers we need to realise that we cannot control the decisions that people make in respect of their own lives, such as leaving work to travel the world. However, we don't have to be thrown into a flat spin when they do. This should be seen as an opportunity rather than a disaster. Theorists advocate that instead of doing everything to avoid instability, we should look to embrace it and ensure that we develop skills and processes that help us to consider, plan for and manage change.

As a manager of people, the challenge is to successfully navigate between stability and instability in order to continually improve the organisation and its employees.

HOW DOES THIS HELP YOU AT WORK?

Understanding that we may find ourselves at the Edge of Chaos can help us to react positively to change. The theory helps to establish that whilst we should look for stability, an organisation will be stronger if it is continuously striving to improve.

It helps by highlighting the need to include continuous improvement and feedback as part of the ongoing training and development of teams and individuals.

WHY IS IT USEFUL?

It is beneficial to know that there is research and thinking to show that change should be seen as an opportunity rather than a threat. Organisations that share this thinking with its employees and adapt to make the most of opportunities to improve, are likely to see changes embraced by the team that lead to increased performance.

Keep your People Management processes and plans under review, and adapt them to meet the changing needs of the organisation.

It can also help to acknowledge when the organisation is moving too close to being chaotic, and recognising the signs of this in the negative behaviour of employees, such as increased absence.

An awareness of managing at the Edge of Chaos helps to reinforce that nothing in life remains static. From a People Management perspective, it shows how continual change at work should be acknowledged and not seen as negative. It illustrates that it is an inescapable aspect of both our working and home lives that should be embraced and managed rather than avoided.

The theories outlined in this chapter are only three out of hundreds that exist and cover a wide range of People Management subjects. Our understanding of the theoretical aspects of people and how to manage them is continually evolving. A fundamental of People Management is People Development (see Chapter 9). Ensure you continue to develop your People Management skills by keeping up to date with current research and thinking.

THE FIVE KEY FACTORS – THREE THEORIES THAT MAKE SENSE

The Five Key Factors embodied by Managers I first described in Chapter 1 can be applied to your approach to People Management theories:

1. *Enthusiasm*

Successful bosses have the drive to keep going in the face of chaos and embrace opportunities for change and improvement.

2. *Open Communication*

The psychological contract illustrates the importance of employee thoughts, feelings and behaviour. Successful managers use regular and open communication methods to gather this information and respond accordingly.

3. *A Head for Business and a Heart for People*

Successful managers balance a fair pay structure with running a profitable organisation. They recognise the sound business sense of fulfilling more than just the basic needs of their teams, as happy settled employees means increased productivity and performance.

4. *Engaging and Empowering*

Fully engaging employees leads to a better understanding of their needs and increased potential for avoiding or managing problems. Engaging employees in a change process will mean they are more likely to embrace and actively work towards achieving it.

5. *Listening and Learning*

Successful managers gather information relating to all external and internal factors influencing their organisation. They seek, listen to and act on feedback from team members. As well as monitoring the results from any changes and from their own actions, they learn from them, and adapt their future behaviour.

SUMMARY – THREE THEORIES THAT MAKE SENSE

The three theories show that people, teams and organisations don't fit into neat boxes and the lives they lead don't remain static.

Reading and learning about theories of the dynamics that impact on the behaviour of individuals and teams will help you manage people and your organisation more effectively, particularly if you remember:

1. **Start by getting the basics right in respect of the financial and psychological contracts and ensure that you keep these under review so they remain effective motivators.**

2. **Plan for what you can within your environment, keep an eye on what is going on outside of it, and be prepared to react and make changes when necessary. Remember that your competitors will be doing the same and you don't want them to catch up or get ahead of you!**

3. **Engage with individuals and teams as regular feedback is vital in developing a high performing team.**

4. **Be prepared to manage the chaos of shifting priorities, people, and teams but ensure that changes are planned, outcomes considered and results reviewed.**

5. **Successful managers understand that effective People Management requires exceeding the basics of the psychological contract and that this can be achieved through the five key factors above.**

In Chapter 5 we'll discuss people management and strategy and how you can use them to develop your competitive advantage.

CHAPTER FIVE

PEOPLE STRATEGY AND MANAGEMENT

"People are our greatest asset" is a phrase I often hear. On the face of it this is a worthy statement for Managers to make about their employees.

Yet when I now hear the phrase, my reaction is one of annoyance. In business a fixed asset register is used to list the values of things it owns that can then be depreciated over time. People are not things that an organisation owns. They are individuals with families, aspirations and feelings; they will experience hope, happiness, sadness and tragedy. Despite what some people may think, the value of people is not something that can be quantified by cost alone and then slowly written off!

Remembering that people are human beings and treating them objectively, ethically, fairly, openly and with compassion is not just the right thing to do, it is also good for business. Happier, settled and less stressed employees are going to be more productive and less disruptive.

I appreciate that by using the 'greatest asset' phrase people are trying to show that they value their employees. Like them you have probably worked out that without people you wouldn't be able to get things done, and your organisation couldn't exist. Don't label people as an asset but do acknowledge that they are an essential part of your organisation. Your organisation couldn't function without people, and properly managed, they are a critical part of your competitive advantage.

You will doubtless face competitors in your line of business and the people you employ can be an advantage you have over them. If your People Strategy includes recruiting and developing a high performing team you have the potential to outperform your competitors. Unfortunately I do come across organisations that only seem to tolerate employees as a necessary evil, and treat them as just a way of getting work done. Unsurprisingly it is these organisations that have to deal with a constant stream of difficult employment issues and high employee turnover.

Some of the organisations claim that their approach to People Management works as they are making a profit, which to them is an indicator that they are operating successfully. I would argue that their organisations would run better, costs would be lower and profit margins much higher, if they had an effective People Strategy that reduced employee turnover. It doesn't take a genius to work out that the need to recruit less often would save time and money, and avoid lost productivity caused by vacancies.

A GOOD PLACE TO START: HAVE A PEOPLE STRATEGY

The first step to having an effective approach to People Management is to have an effective People Strategy. You may think that I would say this because I run a People Management business, but there is a substantial body of research that proves the positive effects of having strategic human resources (HR) practices.

One research project found that in hospitals having an effective People Management approach could literally save lives. The results showed that, after controlling certain factors, mortality rates were improved when a combined range of strategic HR management activities were employed.

The research identified a number of high performance People Management activities that can help an organisation achieve its goals. They included an emphasis on:

- **Competitive pay and benefits**
- **Engagement and empowerment**
- **Learning and development**
- **Performance management**

If you search the myriad sources of information available on strategy planning, the vast majority don't include advice on developing a People Strategy within that plan. Many of them don't mention people at all, (other than a cursory mention to call them a resource and to only work out what they will cost the organisation). Much of the advice advocates setting a strategic direction and writing into the business plan details about products, services or customer offerings. Very few mention writing a People Strategy or information about their employment offering.

At the start of this chapter I talked about how your team is your competitive advantage and throughout this book I talk about how people are unique. A question often asked when discussing marketing as part of a Business Plan is "What is your Unique Selling Point?" There may be a number of unique selling points, but my answer would include that one of the main ones is the people you employ.

Your People Strategy should not be secondary to your Business Plan and should be unique to your organisation. It needs to be an integral part of your overall business strategy, as recognised by the Chartered Institute of Personnel and Development (CIPD), who state on their website:

"It is too simplistic to suggest that strategic human resource management stems from the organisation's business strategy. The two must be mutually informative. The way in which people are managed, motivated and deployed, and the availability of skills and knowledge, will all shape the business strategy."

An effective People Strategy is a plan that sets out your strategic HR goals, how they will be achieved and what resources will be allocated to achieving them.

The plan should include an analysis of the approach, processes, and actions your organisation will follow to develop and implement fundamental strategic HR activities that will help you build a high performing team.

Your People Strategy should cover the what, why and how of recruitment, pay and benefits, engagement and empowerment, developing people and performance management. These People Management fundamentals are discussed in more detail in chapters 6, 7, 8, 9 and 10 respectively.

Remember that 'one size does not fit all' (see Chapter 1). Your People Strategy needs to be developed to meet the requirements of your unique organisation and should not copied from somewhere else!

ONLY IMPLEMENTATION LEADS TO RESULTS

If you are a boss then it is part of your role to deliver your business strategy and therefore your People Strategy. Remember that failure often results from not executing a strategy rather than a bad strategy.

Executing and delivering on your People Strategy means managing people in order to achieve results. Over the years I have been working in People Management I have heard a wide variety of complaints about managing people. They range from employees being their biggest cost, to how running an organisation would be simpler if it didn't have to employ people! Aside from the obvious point of them not having an organisation if it weren't for people, they are missing an opportunity to make bigger profits and to make life easier for themselves if they worked at getting their People Management right.

In most organisations a significant proportion of the running costs will be spent on recruiting and paying employees. As with any business expenditure it is right that you want to see the best possible return on your investment and measure the results of your People Strategy.

A People Strategy will help you optimise your investment in people but quantifying how can be a challenge. For me quantifying a Return On Investment (ROI) from employees, in respect of how much profit is made from the capital invested, creates not only a challenge but also a dilemma.

The challenge is in identifying what measures to use and how appropriate it is to use them. The measures can include monitoring employee turnover, rates of absenteeism, the effectiveness of training and employee surveys.

The problem with ROI, or any other measure, is that it is a snapshot of one element, at one point in time, and cannot accurately reflect the whole picture. For example, a figure for absence rates may significantly jump from one year to the next due to the unavoidable long-term sickness of just one employee.

My dilemma is that the 'head for business' part of me recognises the validity of measures and their importance in monitoring, managing and developing an organisation. However, the 'heart for people' part of me questions why we feel we have to justify what people do in terms of a number or a percentage.

I would argue that no quantitative measure can fully or accurately calculate the actual invaluable contribution to the success of an organisation that is down to its employees. Qualitative measures in the form of surveys can go some way to achieving this and can include feedback from employees about the part they play in the success or failure of teams and the whole organisation.

I accept that we must be able to demonstrate performance if we are going to ask the same of other people and teams. I would advocate the use of the 'KISS' acronym here and look to 'Keep It Simple, Stupid' as information overload can be confusing and time wasting. What is developed should include how we are doing in helping the organisation to achieve its goals and targets. As the main stakeholders of People Management are the people in the organisation, then regularly surveying them is essential.

As with much of the advice in this book, it is down to what is appropriate to the needs of your individual organisation in achieving its goals. As a word of caution, don't focus solely on the figures at the expense of a wider and more comprehensive assessment of the overall picture of the contribution of people.

Regardless of whether or not any measures are used, logic would suggest and research shows, that strategic human resource practices and the effective managing of people will boost an organisations chance of success.

MANAGING PEOPLE AND PEOPLE MANAGEMENT – ARE YOU THE RIGHT PERSON?

Regardless of whether you have a People Strategy, if you employ people there will be a number of day-to-day managing people activities that need to be coordinated, such as essential paperwork. As a minimum these will include activities relating to recruiting and paying your employees (more information on these can be found in Chapters 6 and 7). Employment law also dictates certain minimum requirements in respect of checking and recording details of an employee's right to work in the UK and paying them. Many of these are statutory and can be costly if you get them wrong.

When it comes to managing the employment of people, you don't have to have a dedicated HR department. However, I would strongly recommend that whoever is responsible for the paperwork has strong administration skills. Keep in mind that the best people to administer the paperwork and the processes of managing people are not necessarily the best people managers.

There is a fundamental difference between the administrative tasks of managing people and the actual issues of People Management. Paperwork, pay and contracts are either right or wrong in respect of content and accuracy, and the distinction is usually very clear. People Management issues are rarely clear-cut, and things do not fit neatly into boxes marked right or wrong.

In my experience I have found that someone who wants everything to be perfect and add up with no surprises, will be good at the administrative side of managing people, but less good at managing people issues. However, someone who gets frustrated by paperwork, who recognises that people do not fit neatly into boxes and that things are not often clearly right or wrong, are likely to fare better with the unpredictability of People Management!

I am not saying that people should just be categorised as either managers of the day-to-day, or people managers. The point I am making here is that if you are in charge of people you will need to be prepared to utilise contradictory skill sets.

The initial reaction of many organisations to a People Management issue is to 'write a policy' to address a situation that is giving them concern. This is not always the only way to deal with an issue, and may be missing an underlying problem. When a manager or client gets in touch to say they want a policy written, I ask for more details about why, and hence establish if that is what is really needed, or if it is symptomatic of another problem that needs resolving.

As a boss, regardless of whether or not you employ a specialist to help you, or you have access to a team of HR people, don't fall into the trap of thinking that you can abdicate the day-to-day responsibility of People Management to others.

All managers of people need to be aware of their additional responsibility to learn about and employ People Management skills to help with decision making. At some point you will find yourself having to make a difficult decision involving someone you employ. This sometimes leads to making tough decisions affecting the few to protect the majority thereby ensuring the survival and success of the organisation. Ultimately the organisation has to prevail, as the hard truth is that if the organisation fails there is no employment for anyone.

There is no perfect approach to People Management and it is impossible to expect yourself, or anyone else, to be able to predict and stop problems. As discussed in Chapter 1, the only predictable thing about people is that they are unpredictable. Be prepared to deal with the irrational, emotional and downright flabbergasting things that people will do.

Whilst a People Strategy will not eliminate all problems, having one will certainly help to minimise them and to help you to deal with issues when they do arise.

ONGOING INVESTMENT

In Chapter 4 I made the point that the external environment that impacts on people and organisations isn't static.

I have often seen managers who have fallen into the trap of thinking that once a vacancy is filled everything will be fine and that things will jog along exactly as they planned.

People Management doesn't end with the appointment of an employee, yet in many organisations there will be little investment in effective People Management beyond initial recruitment. Your investment in time, money and effort relating to people starts with planning their recruitment and it keeps going throughout their whole time with you.

A significant part of your role as a boss is to ensure that you, your team and your organisation achieve the objectives of the Business Plan. To maximise your ability to meet those objectives, you should ensure that developing your people is a key part of your People Management activities.

PLANNING TO REACH YOUR GOALS

Getting your People Strategy right will help you to achieve your targets. An inevitable aspect of business planning is regularly reviewing how many people you need, and what you need them to do. Whether you are planning for downsizing, consolidation, or growth, people planning needs to be a fundamental part of this and not an afterthought. Changes in team numbers or job requirements will impact on individuals, teams and the whole organisation.

The place to start planning a change is to review the current status of your organisation. This is not just about your marketplace or what it makes, but also the people in it. As well as thinking about how the business is doing, I recommend that you also regularly ask yourself how you and your team are doing.

Every three to six months allow yourself the time to take stock, and ask a few People Management 'health check' questions, such as:

1. **How are things going against our plans and targets?**

2. **How are people, including me, doing?**

3. **What targets or challenges are coming up?**

4. **Are there any blockers, people or otherwise, that are stopping us, or could stop us from achieving them?**

5. **Do we have the right number of people, or the people with the right skills?**

6. **What do we need to stop doing or do differently?**

These questions can also be asked of your team as part of regular one-to-one, or team meetings. These should be part of your open communication approach integral to the Engagement and Empowerment aspect of your People Management strategy (see Chapter 8). It is just as important to ask the same questions of yourself. You would want your team to tell you about issues they are having and you need to be prepared to be honest with yourself too!

The responses to these questions will help to inform what you need to consider in respect of your People Strategy. This may include meeting training and development needs, or setting and managing performance targets for poor performers. It could involve empowering those who have demonstrated their capabilities by giving them other tasks or greater responsibilities.

If you get to a point when you can't answer the questions satisfactorily, or you are too busy to stop and think about anything, then that is a clear indicator that change is required in the organisation, your People Strategy, or both.

If you are experiencing problems, or are considering expanding or reducing the team, the temptation is to dive in and address what you see as being the immediate issue. The danger is this is a short-term solution and you have missed less obvious, but potentially more important contributing aspects.

Whilst time can be a factor, and it can be tempting to make something happen, it will not help you in the long term if you are perpetually making time-consuming short-term fixes. The more effective approach is to invest the time to collect data and analyse what you are doing, what you need to be doing, and the gaps between the two. This data analysis will also help to develop the plan of how you can bridge the gaps.

An approach that you can use, that can help you achieve your organisational targets and People Strategy, is Organisation Development (OD). This is about embracing and harnessing change to improve not only the day-to-day operation, but also the long-term success of your organisation. It is not a way to shoehorn in a change for change's sake. The driver for any change should be looking at why and how individuals, groups and organisations can be made more effective. It is not about short term, quick fixes. Properly structured OD will allow you to prepare to react to inevitable future evolutions and changes.

Organisation Development brings together theories and practices that can increase the effectiveness of organisations but acknowledges that there needs to be analysis around the unique needs of each organisation. There is no one set way of managing change so beware of anyone who tries to sell you a one-size fits all approach.

From my experience of helping organisations, successful Organisation Development is characterised by applying scientific (and logical) behavioural approaches to gathering and analysing data. This leads to the accurate identification of needs that will shape plans for effective interventions and change.

It is most effective when it involves everyone in the team or organisation and is conducted in an open, objectively challenging and supportive environment.

The overall aim should be the delivery of sustainable improvements to the performance and wellbeing of individuals, teams and the whole organisation.

However, it is also about remembering that success in business is in being strategic, pragmatic and output focused, to ensure that an organisation not only survives but also thrives.

Organisation Development can be an effective part of your Business Plan and People Strategy. If you use the questions above as the basis of a regular Organisation Development health check, you will optimise opportunities for yourself, your team and your organisation to be ready to take on your competitors and future challenges.

THE FIVE KEY FACTORS – PEOPLE STRATEGY AND MANAGEMENT

The Five Key Factors embodied by managers I first described in Chapter 1 can be applied to your approach to your People Strategy:

1. Enthusiasm

Successful people managers have enthusiasm for people, and recognise that the success of an organisation is inextricably linked with the people it employs.

2. Open Communication

Having regular one to ones and asking the People Management 'health check' questions every six months, can lead to the improvement of your People Strategy. Finding out what people think and being open to their thoughts and ideas can help you to improve the performance of individuals and therefore, the whole organisation.

3. A Head for Business and a Heart for People

Successful people managers find a balance between the need to drive performance to achieve the organisation's business plan and investing time and effort into achieving its people plan. To them success is measured not only by profit or ROI figures but also by employee development and satisfaction.

4. Engaging and Empowering

An effective People Strategy includes factors that engage people in their own development so they make more effective decisions that can lead to improved performance. Empowered individuals can also help to support and develop their colleagues, leading to increased effectiveness of the team and the whole organisation.

5. Listening and Learning

Your People Strategy can be developed and improved through listening to your team. They are the ones best placed to give you feedback about the reality of how processes, plans and ideas are actually working.

SUMMARY – PEOPLE STRATEGY AND MANAGEMENT

A People Strategy that covers the fundamentals of People Management will help you to develop a high performing team.

The People Strategy you develop, the approach you take to the everyday management of people, the measures of success you use and how you embrace change, will all be guided by the individuality of people, teams and the whole organisation.

When developing your People Strategy remember:

1. **People are essential to an organisation and form part of your competitive advantage, so have a strategy in place to maximise their performance. Remember that our lives are constantly in a state of flux and as a result your People Management strategy shouldn't sit rigidly in a static state, it should evolve and develop.**

2. **High performance People Management activities including: recruitment, competitive pay and benefits, engagement and empowerment, learning and development and performance management are proven to make a positive difference.**

3. **Measuring success is a balance of using quantitative measures such as profit and ROI, and qualitative measures such as employee surveys.**

4. **Carry out a regular 'health check' of how you, your employees, teams and the whole organisation are doing and make changes where appropriate.**

5. **Learning and development for yourself and the managers in your team should include an awareness of the five key factors of People Strategy and how these can lead to effective People Management.**

In Chapter 6 we'll discuss ways in which you can develop a People Management approach to finding and recruiting a high performing team.

CHAPTER SIX

RECRUITING PEOPLE

In Chapter 5 I stated that the people you employ are part of your competitive advantage. As with many aspects of People Management there is no perfect process that will lead to you appointing the perfect employee. However, you can, as part of your People Strategy, develop an approach to recruitment that will help you appoint high performing people who will maximise your competitive advantage.

Key to this is remembering that recruitment is more than just finding someone with the right skills and experience to do the job. An often overlooked vital element is finding candidates who have the personality and approach to complement and integrate successfully with the rest of the team. Also many organisations lose sight of the crucial fact that recruitment is a two way process. You have to sell your organisation to potential candidates as being the best one to join, just as much as they have to sell themselves to you.

When recruiting, you can't assume that just because you have a job to fill, the right people are readily available and waiting to present themselves to you. Even in an economic downturn when there should be plenty of candidates to choose from, it doesn't automatically follow that the best candidates will apply for your vacancy. To build an effective team, you want to take on the best person for the job, not just someone who can do the job.

If a person is good at what they do and they are settled in their current organisation, you have to make sure that your approach to People Management will be sufficient to tempt them into joining yours.

The following information in this chapter will not set out an exact recruitment process for you to follow. It does identify stages that I have found are critical in building a high performing team. You can use the information to develop a process best suited to your organisation.

A GOOD PLACE TO START: WORKING OUT WHAT YOU NEED

The best place to start is to analyse what has led you to the point of looking to recruit. If you want to fill a new role it will help if you think about the impact it will have on covering particular tasks and duties, and what other roles it can potentially affect. If you are considering recruiting because someone is moving on from an existing job, either because they are leaving or have been promoted, take the opportunity to consider whether you need a 'like for like' replacement. The vacancy could open up an opportunity to give more responsibility to someone already in your team, or to recruit someone with a different skill set.

Regardless of whether you are increasing your headcount or filling a vacancy, the next stage is to identify what needs to be done, what skills and experience you need and how that person needs to fit into your current team. It will help if you engage other people in your team at this stage, including, if applicable, the person who is moving on, to get their thoughts about the requirements of the role. Their input can be useful in ensuring you recruit to meet the team's actual needs.

Once you have decided on the details of the vacancy you want to fill, the next stage is to produce a job description. Over the years I have seen many different examples of what is typically called a Job Description, but can have various titles including Role Profile and Person Specification. There is no set format to any of these and a search online will provide you with hundreds of examples. You can also find interesting articles and blog posts from people arguing that you don't need to have job descriptions at all.

I am not going to debate here what they are called, what goes into them, or even whether you have them or not. It is for you to decide what is appropriate for your particular organisation.

If you do decide to write one then what I would say is, don't be tempted to just copy a job description from elsewhere. Ensure that what you develop meets your organisation's particular requirements and avoid the typical pitfalls that include:

- **It becomes a long 'to do' list.**

- **It is so detailed that it is restrictive and could result in someone saying, "It's not on my job description" when something doesn't get done.**

- **Expecting to recruit someone who will be able to meet the requirements of everything listed in the job description.**

As an aside to job descriptions, I do advocate organisations not getting hung up on job titles. A job is more than a title and it is not possible to convey everything in a role using only a couple of words. If you are developing a role remember that the majority of time should be spent on what it needs to cover, not what it is called.

I also advocate that organisations avoid the traditional organisation chart. I have lost too much time stuck in meetings trying to define a chart that rapidly becomes out of date. Time consuming debates have raged about what lines go where, if they are solid or dotted, how big the box is, and if it should it be higher on the page than the person next to them as they are more senior. I have also then had to spend more time resolving problems when they are published.

The traditional organisation chart can be replaced with a 'who's who' and details about what people do, which is less contentious but is still very useful both for external stakeholders and for new team members during induction.

If you do produce something that defines the role, then you need to make sure it does not over or under sell it. Writing something based on how you want someone to develop rather than focusing on what you want them to do now, can lead to recruiting the wrong person.

Once you have decided on what support you need, the next step is to recruit someone to fill your vacancy.

THERE'S NO 'YOU' IN TEAM

A phrase that always makes my heart sink when consulted about recruitment is "I want to recruit another me". There is no other you – you are unique, so already the task is impossible.

Instead of looking for a 'mini me', take the opportunity to build your high performing team by finding someone to add to the mix of what is already in place. You can look for people with the same skills, work ethic and values as you, but consider what different experience and personality styles they will need to complement or fill gaps in the team.

Research, such as the work of Dr. Meredith Belbin (2010), shows that high performing teams are made up of a mix of styles. Belbin studied the behaviour of teams competing in a business game. The game was part of a 10-week course for successful managers identified as having board level potential.

It was thought that the likely outcome of the game would be that high-intellect teams would perform better than the lower intellect ones. In fact he found that some teams that were expected to be successful, based on high intellect, failed to fulfil their predicted potential. It was not intellect, but the mix of a team and the compatibility of roles that members played, that helped the team to be successful

Belbin identified nine distinctive and useful team roles. He also found that whilst a range of different behaviours is essential to team success, the key to success is balance. Too few or too many of a particular role, can create issues such as a lack of creative ideas, missing deadlines, and too much infighting.

Each role is important in ensuring that the team functions at an optimum level and there is no 'best' type. As the roles are linked to personality, people perform better in roles that come more naturally to them. This means that as individuals we should not try to be something we are not and shouldn't try to force people into roles unsuited to their personalities.

The challenge is in identifying the personality and team styles in your current employees and potential recruits, as well as working out if there are gaps and how to fill them.

There are various tests that can be used as part of identifying team roles, however, their use must be considered carefully. Whilst they can be useful as part of a programme of team building and personal development, they are not always suitable to use as a recruitment tool. There are personality profile tests that have been specifically designed for use in a recruitment process and a search online will bring up a range to choose from. Avoid using an untested and non-validated tool. For more information on validated tests, go to the British Psychological Society's Psychological Testing Centre web site at www.psychtesting.org.uk.

If a test is used, it should only form part of a detailed, open, fair and robust process, and should never be used as the only method of recruitment. It should also be available in alternative formats so that it does not discriminate against candidates with a special need or disability.

INTERNAL AND EXTERNAL

The first stage of your recruitment process should always be to consider whether you could fill the vacancy internally.

It may be an obvious point but before you start your search for candidates outside of your organisation, check to see if the best person for the job is already in your team by advertising the job internally. Even if you believe there isn't a suitable internal candidate, you should always internally advertise the role. Otherwise you risk having disgruntled and demotivated employees complaining about not being given a fair opportunity to apply for a role they were interested in.

If your People Management approach includes investing in training and development, it may be that someone is ready for their next move. Having regular one-to-ones with your team will help. If you include training and development as a regular aspect of your discussions, you should already be aware of who might be ready to step into the role.

A consequence of openly advertising internally is that you may receive applications from employees you don't think are suited to the role. This should not be seen as a problem if you ensure that all internal candidates go through an open, fair and robust recruitment process.

The recruitment process for internal or external applicants should include assessing whether the candidate will be able to perform effectively and meet the requirements of their new role, regardless of their performance in their current role.

In their book The Peter Principle: Why Things Always Go Wrong, Laurence Peter and Raymond Hull (1969) set out their management theory whereby an employee rises "to the level of their incompetence". They describe how the tendency is to promote people on the basis of performance in their current job until they are appointed into a role in which they fail.

A robust recruitment process will help to demonstrate to internal candidates that even if they are successful in their current role, it is not a given they will be appointed unless they can prove their ability meet the requirements of the new role.

If the employee is not appointed, it can provide objective evidence for feedback to illustrate where their skills and experience were not suitable for the role. This can subsequently help with planning a discussion about how to assist them with training and coaching to support the personal development needed for them to achieve their future ambitions.

Remember, as discussed in Chapter 3, you are looking to appoint or promote the person best suited to a role and not just the longest serving, the most skilled, or the one with the highest intellect!

FINDING THE NEEDLE IN THE HAYSTACK

Recruitment is not an exact science and there is no perfect process guaranteed to find the right person every time.

I have experienced many situations where, after following a thorough recruitment process it seems as if we have found the perfect employee, but after they join the alchemy just doesn't work out. This often manifests in performance issues. (See Chapter 10 on how to manage performance.)

From experience I have found that the best way to minimise potential recruitment problems, is to have a robust and open process. It should include a number of stages, and involve some or all of the team with whom the candidate will be working. The overriding aim should be to develop a process that gives all parties a fair opportunity to learn as much as they can about each other, so that the most effective decisions can be made. If candidates 'deselect' themselves from the process because they can see that the organisation or role is not right for them, it will save time for all concerned.

To ensure fairness, the process should be the same for all candidates, although the finer detail of interview questions can vary where appropriate. Internal candidates should be expected to apply and follow the same process as everyone else. However, it is sensible to make some adjustments as appropriate. For example, it will not be useful to ask the classic "Tell us about your current role" question in an interview with an internal applicant!

Where possible the recruitment process should involve more than one interviewer. This can help to avoid accusations of bias particularly in respect of internal applicants. If the internal candidate gets the job, it is helpful to be able to demonstrate that it was due to merit and not favouritism.

If internal sources are unlikely to yield suitable applicants then you need to look to fill the vacancy through other routes. These can include a temporary or permanent appointment using a recruitment agency, or by advertising externally. Whatever your chosen route, I advocate having the same process for advertising and recruitment.

GOING EXTERNAL

If you are placing the role with an agency or doing it yourself by advertising externally, you need to give as much detail as possible including salary. This will help to avoid potential problems in the later stages of the process. Don't advertise a salary to tempt people in the hope that you can get away with trying to negotiate less later on, or quote a low figure to see what you can get away with paying. It is important to advertise a market rate salary - even in tough economic times; good quality candidates know their worth.

Don't under or over sell the job in the advert. Whilst you may have good intentions to give an opportunity for development, it will only lead to resentment if it doesn't subsequently materialise.

Placing an advert online is a time and cost effective way of advertising your vacancy. It only takes a couple of clicks to send off a CV for a job so it also makes the application process easier for candidates. The downside of this is that you can find yourself with hundreds of applications to work through. Many of these will be from people who are not seriously interested in your job but thought they would apply to see what happens.

A good way of testing people to see if they are really interested in your job is to set a task linked to the potential role as part of the application process. For example, if the job is for a Product Manager, you may want them to submit a one-page product proposal. If you receive applications from people who haven't bothered to do this, it acts as the first objective measure for rejecting an application.

Don't forget that you are looking to impress the best candidates so they are motivated to join your organisation. So as well as being courteous, acknowledging the receipt of all applications and making it clear how candidates will know if their application has been successful or not, creates a good first impression of your organisation as being a being a thoughtful employer.

Creating a good impression of your organisation as polite and professional, even with unsuccessful candidates, is not only the right thing to do but it may help you in the future. Whilst the applicant may not be suitable on this occasion they may be ideal for another role you advertise.

The next stage is to read the applications and compare the applicant's skills and experience against what you require for the role, and thereby identify a shortlist of people to interview.

Once you have your applicants reduced to a shortlist the next stage is to develop a process that will identify the best person for the job. As I have said earlier in this chapter, recruitment is not an exact science; there is no perfect indicator or tool that will accurately predict the potential of candidates to succeed in a role.

Research carried out by Stephen Taylor (1988) showed that if perfect prediction is deemed to be 1.0, then the accuracy of one-to-one interviews is very low and rates between 0.1 and 0.2. The best predictor is achieved by carrying out assessment centres which rate at between 0.6 and 0.7.

An assessment centre is a term used for a process where a number of candidates are brought together at the same time to complete different work based tasks. They may include oral and written tests such as presentations and in-tray exercises; they often include both individual and group tasks.

Assessment centres are not always practical for small organisations but irrespective of the size of your organisation, you can develop a process along similar lines that is appropriate to your size of organisation.

A TWO STAGE PROCESS

My recommendation is that your recruitment process has a minimum of two stages. Whilst time may be pressing and you need to get someone on board, investing the time into more than one interview stage can save you problems in the future.

Having at least two stages will enable you to gather more information about the candidates. The first stage should be designed to check the skills, experience and abilities that candidates state on their application, and other information you ask them to submit. It also gives you the opportunity to see if they have done their homework about the role and your organisation.

As part of the first interview you may want to consider asking candidates to prepare and deliver a short presentation on a subject related to the role. Other options include practical exercises such as preparing a response to a letter, examining a set of figures or information for accuracy, or proof reading a document.

The aim is to whittle the candidate numbers down for the second and more challenging stage.

A two stage process can help ensure that you gather a wide range of information about potential candidates. It can also help highlight behaviour differences from one meeting to the next. I have seen strong candidates become over confident in the second interview, and conversely a weaker candidate excel in the second interview after they have overcome their initial nerves.

In the second interview you can plan questions based on scenarios the candidates may be required to tackle in the role, to see how they react and plan their approach. They may also be able to offer practical examples of their experience. One of my clients plans the second interviews around their values statement, and asks candidates for their thoughts on, and examples of, their approach geared around those values.

At the second stage I recommend that you include personality or team style profiling to give an indication of the likely fit with the rest of the team. At some point during the two stages I strongly encourage involving other people from the team and asking them what they think about the candidates. Team members can give interviewees a tour of the building and can then contribute their feedback. As well as giving team members the opportunity to assess the candidates they are likely to be working with, it enables the applicants to find out directly what it is like to work for the organisation.

TELL ME MORE – INTERVIEWING

Before embarking on interviews, if you have not been on an interviewing training course then I recommend attending one to avoid potential pitfalls. It will not define the exact method for your interviews but it will increase your chances of selecting the most suitable candidate.

An element to remember about interviews is that they are also an opportunity for candidates to test you out. The high performing candidates who are looking for their next opportunity are likely to be applying for a number of roles and may have other interviews in the pipeline. The interview is your opportunity to show to them why they should choose to join you. If you turn the interview into an interrogation with questions designed to trip candidates up, then they are not likely to want to join your organisation. Remember too that with the advent of social media, people can easily share their experiences of bad interviews, which may lead to other people being put off applying to your organisation.

I have come across many managers who think they are a good judge of character and only need to interview someone once as they go with their 'gut reaction'. They may be able to point to previous successes, but when you dig deeper, they are also often the ones with a string of employee issues behind them.

Research shows that we make decisions on people very quickly when first meeting them; it also shows how inaccurate these first impressions can be. My advice is that if you have a 'gut feel' about an interview candidate then make sure that you are asking questions during the interview that will either prove or disprove your gut. This is also a good reason to have more than one person interviewing, as you can challenge each other's perceptions of a candidate's performance.

One of the main things to remember about an interview process is that it is not guaranteed that you will find someone. If this is the case don't panic and make an appointment on the basis of the best of a bad bunch, or the misguided optimism that you can eventually shape someone into what you want.

Consider covering the role temporarily. Take time to think about the quality of the candidates you have seen and critically evaluate whether information about the job and in the advert is accurate. You should also carefully consider whether you advertised in the best places.

Whilst there are no recruitment guarantees, you can increase your potential for success by having a process that is open, ethical, fair and robust, which includes a number of stages and tests, and involves more than one assessor.

THE FIVE KEY FACTORS – RECRUITING PEOPLE

The Five Key Factors embodied by managers I first described in Chapter 1 can be applied to your approach to recruiting people:

1. Enthusiasm

Being enthusiastic about your organisation and what it does will impress potential candidates that it is an organisation they want to join.

2. Open Communication

Advertising internally and externally will maximise the potential to make the best appointment. Open communication includes talking to the current team, and giving candidates every opportunity to find out if this is the job and organisation for them.

3. A Head for Business and a Heart for People

Whilst you can look to help develop internal people and give them a chance; you need to be pragmatic about making the best decision for the organisation. Ultimately it is not helpful to the appointed person if sentimentality gets the better of you, and they are over promoted and hence fail. You are looking for the best person for the job; an open and pragmatic process will help you achieve this.

4. Engaging and Empowering

Engage the rest of the team in the recruitment process. As well as improving the odds of appointing the right person, it will begin the process of building lines of communication that will integrate the appointee into the team.

5. Listening and Learning

Input from the team will be invaluable in identifying what and who you need to include, to ensure that the team and organisation are successful.

SUMMARY – RECRUITING PEOPLE

Recruitment is not an exact science and not every appointment you make will be successful but an open, fair and robust process will minimise the risk of getting it wrong. An effective recruitment strategy with a process that covers internal and external applicants will help you find and appoint a high performing team. Remember:

1. **Take time to work out what and whom you need and involve others who will be working with them.**

2. **You are not just looking for competency and skill – just as important is the overall fit with rest of the team.**

3. **Develop an open and robust process that has more than one stage and includes testing skills, experience, personality and fit with the team and keeps in mind that you need to impress potential candidates just as much as they need to impress you.**

4. **A carbon copy of you or someone else, the longest serving, or the most intelligent or technically competent person is not automatically the best person for the job.**

5. **As the boss make sure you are following the five key factors with respect to the recruitment process.**

In Chapter 7 we'll discuss an approach to pay that will help both in the recruitment of new employees and in motivating current employees.

CHAPTER SEVEN

PAY AND BENEFITS

Assuming your employees are not eccentric millionaires who work for the fun of it, the main motivating factor that drives them to work is not love for your organisation or product; it's the salary that you pay them. You can make your organisation the most exciting and fun place to work but if you are not paying the going rate for salary and benefits, you will lose people to competitors that are.

The constant challenge when running an organisation is to be solvent, hopefully with a surplus to show a profit and allow opportunities for investment in growth and development. A substantial cost for any organisation is what you pay yourself and your employees. An effective organisation needs to have in place a fair, transparent and objective Pay and Benefits strategy.

There is nothing more emotive to people than pay. Money provides people the means to pay for food and shelter. In a work context, it can help employees meet the physiological and social needs that are the first two levels of Maslow's Hierarchy of Needs (see Chapter 4). The right strategy for paying people is integral to building a high performing team.

A Pay and Benefits strategy can range from offering a basic salary and minimal benefits, to a complex system of pay, benefits and bonuses. Beware the temptation that comes from reading or hearing about what works for another organisation and trying to impose it on yours. It is essential that whatever Pay and Benefits strategy you implement, it is developed to meet the needs of your individual organisation.

You may work in a unionised environment where there is collective negotiation with employee representatives or it is non unionised and negotiation is with individuals. Whilst the mechanics of negotiation around pay may differ, the fundamental principles outlined in this chapter are the same for any organisation.

The wrong strategy, or no strategy, leads to poor performance, stress, confrontation, high employee turnover and low morale, which in turn leads to compromised organisation performance.

The information in this chapter will not set out a perfect structure for Pay and Benefits guaranteed to suit your organisation. It will provide you with the basis for developing a remuneration package to reward your employees for the work they deliver.

A GOOD PLACE TO START: WHAT ARE PEOPLE WORTH?

One approach to reward that in my experience doesn't work, is trying to pay what you can get away with. Whilst it might appear to save you money, it is a false economy. Poor pay results in poor performance. If you don't pay competitive market rates you will need to factor in extra costs incurred and time lost from; correcting mistakes, doing more work yourself, customer dissatisfaction, reduced product value and more employee training. All of which results in total costs far greater than paying a competitive salary. You will also find yourself in the position of playing 'catch up' as you will lose employees to organisations that pay the going rate. If your organisation develops a reputation for poor pay and high employee turnover, it will make recruitment more difficult.

Despite what employees may like to think, pay is not based on how nice someone is or if they turn up on time everyday with a smile on their face. An effective approach to pay begins with ensuring that basic salaries are fair and accurately reflect the work that an employee is delivering.

An approach to basic pay that works effectively is where employers have a policy of determining pay by objectively benchmarking basic salaries against prevailing market rates. They are transparent and open about what these are, and have a process through which basic salaries can be reviewed. To be effective this strategy, and the pay rates, need to be compared regularly with rates paid outside and inside the organisation.

Establishing a market rate salary is not difficult to do. The process involves gathering and analysing objective salary data on external pay rates in organisations of a similar size, sector and geographical location. The accuracy of a market rate is dependent on the accuracy of information about the role. Care has to be taken that comparable roles are based on job content, and not just on job title, as these will vary from employer to employer.

An upper and lower band is identified from the salary data within which the salary for roles can be set. Having a lower and upper range for the salary band allows for flexibility of pay between employees if they are carrying out comparable roles but there are measurable differences in responsibility. However, some jobs may be so particular to your organisation that it is difficult to find comparators to measure against. If this is the case then elements of the job role will need to be compared to a range of like roles.

Regardless of what process you use, it should be remembered that there is no formula that will give you an exact and indisputable rate of pay for a role.

WHY ARE THEY GETTING PAID MORE THAN ME?

Your overall pay strategy should ensure that employees doing the same or similar roles receive the same pay. If not, you risk facing disgruntled employees and potentially costly legal action. Equal pay or discrimination claims are messy, time consuming and expensive. They can include gender, ethnicity, age or disability and are a matter of public record. So distrust and ill feeling can spread amongst those directly involved, throughout your organisation and beyond.

Don't fall into the trap of thinking that people don't talk about money or won't ask each other what they earn – I know from experience that they do. You can even ask that people keep their pay details secret, but I have seen plenty of examples where this approach has backfired spectacularly. I have also had to deal with the fallout of matters being made worse when fumbled attempts to justify the difference in pay has led to people raising grievances.

You may be able to justify paying a lower rate if you are taking a gamble on appointing someone less experienced but who shows potential. When they are appointed they should still be paid the market rate for the skills they have at the time. Regardless of their age or length of service, it is equally important that their pay is reviewed once they have developed the same, or better level of skills and experience than someone else doing the equivalent job.

Don't think that the way around this is to give people different job titles. The Equality and Human Rights Commission (EHRC) produces information and guidance aimed at helping employers to implement equal pay within their organisation in accordance with equal pay legislation. The EHRC guidance sets out that people doing like work should be paid equally, regardless of gender and that equal pay is not about looking at performance, it is about assessing job demands.

AN OPEN APPROACH

A significant factor in an effective pay strategy is to openly publish pay rates. If your strategy is to pay a competitive market rate, you have nothing to hide. You can be open with your team and open with your job advertising. This will increase your chances of appointing the best person. If the salary range is made clear in the job advert you are more likely to attract candidates with the right skill level. Also, your chosen candidate is more likely to accept an offer you make.

Whilst an effective pay strategy helps to reduce salary issues, there may still come a time when an employee wants to talk about their level of pay. Your pay strategy should include a process by which job roles can be objectively reviewed. This process should take into account possible increases in the skill level, decision-making or responsibilities within a job, to ensure the basic pay remains competitive with the market rate.

For one of my clients I have developed a process where employees can request a review of their salary by providing objective reasons and evidence to support their request. This has to be supported by their line manager and focuses on establishing demonstrable changes in the level of skill, decision-making or responsibility. The employee is asked to provide supporting evidence including an updated job description that highlights areas of the role that have changed. This is used to benchmark the salary against market rates to determine if an increase is justified.

HOW MUCH IS ENOUGH?

Even after an objective salary review an employee may still disagree with the rate that they are being paid. You must decide whether you will take further action, or if you will leave it to see what action the employee takes. They can of course choose to leave to find a role that pays better elsewhere. If they hand in their notice then you do have the option of making them an increased offer but in my experience, this is likely to generate more problems than it solves. It can create a pay disparity with other employees and lead to their pay becoming overinflated and above the market rate. Having set the precedence of an unwarranted increase, you will potentially have to keep dealing with the same problem as the employee is likely to return again asking for more. You could ultimately end up with a significantly overpaid employee who is also demotivated when you don't continue to increase their pay on demand.

In this situation I suggest it is more than just the salary that needs to be examined. Look to identify what is driving the reason for their continued request, and establish if you are realistically ever able to meet the employee's demands. Review the work they are delivering and the level of responsibility they are operating at, and double check that your market rate salary is accurate. It may mean deciding that, regardless of them being an effective and high performing employee, their request is unrealistic and cannot be met.

An option is to ask the employee to provide examples of jobs they have seen advertised with higher rates, to see if your and their research is looking at comparative roles. This is also a good tip if you are looking to request a salary increase yourself! Basing an argument for increased pay on objective evidence is more powerful than saying you think you should be paid more as you work harder than anyone else. Make sure that you can provide salary details of a range of comparable jobs advertised by employers of a similar size, sector and geographical location. Ensure that these are comparative roles in terms of level of responsibility, decision-making, skill level and competence.

If you have carried out thorough research on comparative salary rates and are confident that the pay is competitive, you may decide to stand your ground. (This is easier to do if you if you keep in mind that a key aspect of managing your team or organisation is that its continued success should not be wholly dependent on the work of one employee).

You can consider discussing alternatives with the employee as to how they can look to eventually earn a higher salary such as how they can achieve promotion. This can include developing their role through job enrichment (see Chapter 9) which involves taking on more responsibility or increasing their levels of skill. This can be easier in larger organisation with different departments, sites or job levels, but is more of a challenge for smaller organisations.

Whatever the size of the team or organisation, you will have to accept that people move on to other departments or employers. If this is because you have a proactive approach to training and personal development and not because your pay and benefits are poor, it is a positive selling point of your organisation that you can use when recruiting their replacement.

YOU WANT MORE?

An important aspect of your pay strategy is to ensure that basic pay is fair and competitive. You will also need to ensure that salaries keep pace with the market rate and your competitors.

Over the years I have seen organisations attempt this using various processes with varied results. The processes have included awarding an annual percentage increase often based on the prevailing Retail Price Index (RPI), having pay spines where salaries increase at a fixed rate over a set time period, and increases linked to annual appraisals.

Inevitably there are downsides with all of these, including salaries becoming over inflated, pay increases being given regardless of the level of performance and inequity of pay between team members.

As a boss the challenge is to work out how to ensure that pay does not demotivate employees, but there are no set methods that can guarantee this.

There are consulting organisations that offer services to develop and implement pay and reward systems. These usually take the form of job evaluation systems based on assessing individual roles and setting out what people need to do in order to influence opportunities to increase pay.

You may have one or more processes in place that you want to change, or are thinking of introducing one. My advice would be to avoid just copying what a competitor does. Carefully research different approaches and talk to managers in other organisations to learn from their experience of the realities of what may be a good idea in theory.

I would advocate keeping things simple. In my experience the most effective approach is to have in place a simple, open and fair approach to establishing, monitoring and increasing pay based on market rates and offering a competitive range of benefits.

THE BENEFITS OF BENEFITS

A fundamental aspect of your pay strategy will be the value to employees of any benefits you decide to offer as part of an overall remuneration package.

Benefits take many forms. They can be financial such as paying the cost of insurances to cover private healthcare, life assurance and long-term sickness, or can enhance the employment experience such as flexible working hours.

One benefit you will have to offer, if you don't do so already, is a workplace pension scheme. Since April 2014 there have been obligations on employers to automatically enrol certain employees into a pension scheme and to make contributions towards it. More information on employer obligations regarding pensions can be obtained from The Pensions Regulator at www.ThePensionsRegulator. gov.uk.

Other than offering access to a pension and statutory obligations such as sick pay, there is no requirement for an employer to offer additional benefits. However, having a range of benefits can be useful in attracting new people and maintaining the wellbeing of existing employees. Some organisations offer 'cafeteria' style benefits where people have an allowance to 'spend' on benefits and can choose from a range offered.

What you offer and how, will be down to a combination of what the organisation can afford, what is useful to employees and what can help you remain competitive in the recruitment market. It doesn't mean that you have to offer exactly the same range of benefits as your competitors. Being creative and offering something different can be more inviting to potential recruits.

One thing to keep in mind is that the value to employees of a particular benefit will differ from person to person. It may be important to you to be able to contribute to a pension but it may not be of interest to someone who has just started work and wants to 'spend' their benefits allowance on something else, such as buying extra holiday.

With benefits you need to consider whether or not they are the same for everyone in respect of qualifying periods and the value of the benefit. I advocate that benefits should be fair to all. Tiers of benefits where the Chief Executive or senior managers get proportionally more value than other employees, in my opinion, isn't completely fair. A Chief Executive's level of responsibility and decision-making should be reflected in their salary. Just because an employee is higher up the organisation doesn't automatically mean they put more effort, care and pride into their work to achieve the organisations goals.

There are individuals and organisations that are remuneration experts. It may save you time, a lot of money and demotivated employees if you consult one of these when considering new, or reviewing existing, Pay and Benefits. Whatever your approach to Pay and Benefits, ensure that it includes asking the team for their input. It can save you time and money if you know what benefits people really want rather than assuming they will want the same as you.

Fundamental to a Pay and Benefits strategy is to; work out what fits your budget, meet any statutory obligations, reassure current and future employees that you are a fair and supportive employer, and be competitive in the recruitment market.

THE BONUS SECTION!

So we come to the subject of bonuses, which in my experience is the aspect of a Pay and Benefits strategy that is the most contentious, time consuming and potentially demotivating.

In this book bonuses include payment made additional to salary (but not overtime or holiday pay) and paid at a frequency from weekly to annually. Bonuses are usually linked to targets and can be known as incentive schemes or performance related pay.

During my years in People Management I have seen an array of bonus schemes that vary in how much is paid and what criteria triggers payment. A common factor is that bonus schemes are usually based on individual, team or organisation performance targets, or a combination of all three.

On an individual level incentives are usually offered as a reward for achieving specific targets. These are based on one, or a range of measures, such as sales targets, productivity figures or achieving personal performance goals.

Team based incentive schemes can cover a sub unit within an organisation, for example different branches in a chain of shops, or different shifts in a production plant. Team bonuses are usually triggered by, and measured against, output targets such as sales, customer satisfaction figures or items produced.

Another incentive type is one that is organisation based. The idea is that everyone shares a common bonus irrespective of role, based on the performance of the organisation. It can promote the concept of unity, and bond the different groups within an organisation. An often quoted example is the John Lewis Partnership in which everyone receives an annual payment that is a percentage of their salary depending on the overall performance of the organisation.

BONUSES – YES OR NO?

I am often asked whether an organisation should pay bonuses. I usually respond by asking why they are considering doing so, thereby prompting a more detailed review of their reasoning and expectations to determine if they are realistic. There are usually two responses; wanting to achieve greater performance, or wanting to share the success of an organisation.

If the response is about wanting better performance from employees then I would question why they are under performing. It could be argued that having a bonus scheme on top of salary as a motivator to achieve desired performance, indicates to employees an expectation that the salary they receive is given for minimum performance. If there is a performance issue, it should be tackled differently to rewarding them with the opportunity to earn more money.

The challenge with any type of bonus scheme is to motivate and reward desired performance, but it is not unknown that they can have the opposite effect.

There is debate about the positive and negative effects of bonus schemes. Research shows that linking pay to performance can actually demotivate people. This is a subject that Daniel Pink covers effectively in his book 'Drive: The surprising truth about what motivates us' (2011) and in online TED (Technology, Entertainment and Design) talks (see References). Pink cites examples of research that demonstrates 'carrot and stick' approaches to pay designed to increase motivation or creativity reduce rather than increase performance. For example how motivating is it if a bonus scheme offers an opportunity to earn up to 30% of annual salary, but in reality no one ever achieves more than 15%?

If you are considering introducing a bonus scheme think carefully about all aspects of it before you do. I have seen many examples where well intentioned but hastily introduced bonus schemes have caused problems including discrimination, team disputes, and lost time and money in resolving claims and complaints.

In respect of discrimination you might consider setting the production of 10 widgets an hour as normal performance, and therefore propose paying a bonus to someone who can produce 12 or more. This might work for some individuals but what about those who are physically unable to work faster to achieve the higher target? Also, if they become demoralised as a result, their production could actually fall and your overall output could be reduced.

In extreme cases, poorly thought out incentive schemes can encourage destructive behaviour. This was exemplified by banking bonus schemes that encouraged aggressive trading that lost banks millions of pounds and brought them to the brink of bankruptcy. The schemes encouraged individuals to chase increasingly risky investments in order to achieve huge personal bonus payouts.

Team incentives are used to avoid only focusing on individual targets and to stimulate performance by creating team targets. This can result in demoralised employees if one team always outperforms another. Teams can also become dysfunctional if blame is put on an individual for reducing group performance. You can find your ability to manage the overall organisation is hindered, for example your attempts to improve output from a low performing team could be hampered by employees' reluctance to move into a group less likely to achieve bonus targets.

With any bonus or performance related pay scheme it is highly likely that you will find yourself in situations where people 'haggle' over the amount of their bonus, including how it compares to someone else's. Yes, people do talk about their bonus as well as their salary, and they think they work harder or perform better than everyone else.

As a minimum a successful scheme will need robust and very clear objective setting, fair assessment of what are often subjective targets and regular meetings to assess performance against targets. You will also need to allow for possible adjustment of targets during the year to take into account unexpected issues that are not the fault of either the employee or the organisation. Clear, unequivocal and fair criteria for different situations need to be planned to cover external factors such as market rate changes and economic challenges and internal circumstances such as probation periods, disciplinary issues, long-term illness and maternity and paternity leave. Even then be prepared for the possibility that you will find yourself spending time reviewing individual cases.

If you are considering an incentive scheme, ask yourself searching questions about why. Is it a genuine desire to share in success or is it about trying to use incentives to fix a problem?

Before you change or introduce any bonus scheme, I recommend you review research about how incentives can be demotivating, and critically evaluate the pros and cons for all schemes being considered.

If you have or are intent on introducing a bonus scheme then be prepared to invest time setting up, running and managing it, as well as mediating disputes and dealing with disgruntled employees!

GET THE BASICS RIGHT

In Chapter 1 of this book, I said that good managers demonstrate and follow the values of being objective, ethical, open, fair and compassionate. It should be evident from the analysis so far that there is a risk that pay, benefits and bonus schemes can contravene one or more of these critical criteria.

The starting point for any scheme is that every employee has the right to know the range of pay for the work they do and what they need to do to improve their performance and hence their pay.

If you have done thorough research to ensure that pay and benefits are competitive, are setting realistic targets and regularly monitoring them, then you should be securing the performance that you want. If you want more performance, then you have to first ask if this is realistic and fair; and also ask if it should be part of the day-to-day aspect of the role. If it is, then the answer may be to look at the basic salary rather than introducing a bonus or performance related pay scheme.

If you have employees that you feel are under performing take time to reflect. Are they the right employee? Have you provided them with adequate training? Have you properly communicated what is expected from them? These and other related aspects of People Management are covered elsewhere in this book.

As mentioned at the outset of this chapter, pay is one of the most emotive aspects of People Management. Don't expect to please all of the people all of the time. However, the good news is that the best approach isn't a secret and doesn't have to be complicated. Keep it simple, pay a fair and competitive market rate, have an objective process for reviewing salaries, find out what benefits are really of value to your team and think very carefully before offering bonuses.

THE FIVE KEY FACTORS – PAY AND BENEFITS

The Five Key Factors embodied by managers I first described in Chapter 1 can be applied to your approach to Pay and Benefits:

1. Enthusiasm

For ensuring an equitable and open process that fairly remunerates people for the work they are delivering.

2. Open Communication

The open communication of salary data and processes for how employees can influence their earning potential will help ensure you are aware of and can look to tackle potentially demotivating issues.

3. A Head for Business and a Heart for People

Using objective pay and benefits information will mean that you are doing the right thing in providing a remuneration package that acknowledges a fair days pay for a fair days work. This is good for business in that it can reduce costly employee turnover and performance issues, and be an effective approach to managing what is a high cost to your organisation.

4. Engaging and Empowering

Engaging with the team will help to identify pay issues as well as ensuring that what you are offering is what people really want. Empowering people, as part of the process of salary reviews will help them to see and understand that pay is established as part of a fair and objective process.

5. Listening and Learning

Listen to what employees think about pay, benefits and bonuses. This will help you to learn if you are getting them right and can help save you time, money and stress if you are not!

SUMMARY – PAY AND BENEFITS

Getting pay and benefits right is fundamental to ensuring that you can attract, motivate and retain the people who can help you to drive the success of your organisation.

Having an effective Pay and Benefits strategy is not complicated if you remember:

1. **Establish accurate and competitive market rates and be prepared to pay them.**

2. **Determine what benefits employees want, balance this with what your competitors are offering and what you can realistically afford, and apply them fairly to all.**

3. **Don't use bonuses to try to correct underperformance. Think very carefully and research all of the advantages and potential pitfalls of introducing, changing or removing a bonus scheme.**

4. **Be open and clear about salary, rewards and targets and remember that people will talk and share what they are paid or what bonus they have received.**

5. **An approach that follows the Five Key Factors will help you to develop a simple, fair and effective pay and benefits strategy.**

In Chapter 8 we look at how engaging with and empowering your team can ensure they are performing the right task, at the right time and to the right standard.

CHAPTER EIGHT

ENGAGEMENT AND EMPOWERMENT

In earlier chapters I talked about recruiting people and having a strategy to manage them. The reason we recruit people is no more complicated than needing them to work in return for pay. As the boss your role is to ensure your team members are doing what they need to do, when it is needed, to the required standard, and in line with your organisation's goals.

You could manage people by telling them exactly what to do, and then watching them all of the time to ensure that they do it. Whilst this might get things done, it is highly probable it will be an unpleasant experience for everyone, including you. Such controlling behaviour implies to people that they cannot be trusted and have to be watched to avoid shirking. I have come across some managers who have behaved like this. Fortunately, the incidences have been rare, but they are memorable, not least because these have been the most unsuccessful, unpopular and ineffective managers I have seen. They think they are taking charge and managing with a firm hand, but in reality they are ineffective and behaving like a bully.

Such an oppressive approach has a human cost; it creates an environment that is unpleasant and stressful. The cost to an organisation can be even greater. As well as being time consuming, it is likely to stifle creativity and motivation, and lead to high employee turnover, poor performance, lost productivity and tribunal settlements.

The challenge for any boss is to motivate and inspire their team to achieve the organisation's goals by delivering work on time, to budget and to the required standard.

In Chapter 5 I illustrated how having a People Management strategy can help achieve your organisation's goals. The strategy involves developing a range of strategic human resource activities, which includes Engagement and Empowerment. Engaging with and empowering the members of your team is an essential part of motivating them.

A GOOD PLACE TO START:
ENGAGING AND EMPOWERING – WHAT'S THE DIFFERENCE?

Engaging people at work is about creating the conditions within which your team members' interest and attention is focused on delivering the requirements of their role, as well as team and organisation targets. This includes involving them in decisions which impact on all of these. If you engage with your team members and have regular meaningful contact with them, they are more likely to share ideas or concerns with you. Not only will this lead to improvements in the performance of the individual but it can benefit the wider team and whole organisation.

Empowering people means giving them the knowledge, responsibility and support to have control over what they do and how they do it. It can lead to improved results and better performance, as they don't have to keep stopping to ask you what to do. Employees will come to know their role better than anyone. This knowledge and experience can be used to increase their effectiveness and confidence in decision-making. An additional benefit is that their skills and experience can be utilised in training others, helping to build a more effective team.

The research discussed in Chapter 5 on improving mortality rates in hospitals supports the benefits of Engagement and Empowerment. It showed that nurses who were consulted at work, well trained, and given more autonomy to make decisions, were more likely to collaborate effectively and share knowledge with others. The overall results concluded that practices that actively encourage and support Engagement and Empowerment have a positive impact on mortality rates.

Engaging and Empowering employees does not mean that you have to be completely egalitarian, involving them in or telling them about everything, or letting them do exactly what they want. It is also not devolving all decisions and responsibility. There still needs to be someone who is acknowledged as having the final say on direction, objectives, quality standards and outputs. It would be naïve to think that Engagement and Empowerment will mean that no mistakes are ever made. Managers themselves need to be empowered to resolve problems, and to advise on issues or disputes between team members. As will be illustrated in Chapter 10, conflict is an aspect of all teams, high performing or otherwise, and someone may need to act as referee!

EARLY APPROACHES TO ENGAGEMENT

There are some radical commentators on people and motivation who would argue that the term 'manager' is outdated. Their argument is that this harks back to the days of Victorian factory owners who controlled many aspects of their employees' lives. During the Victorian period even the more altruistic of employers thought that their poorly educated workers needed to be told what to do, and when to do it, as they were not capable of looking after themselves.

Whilst this was a misguided approach, we can look back and see that even if it was inadvertent, Victorian factory owners were early pioneers of what we today call Engagement and Empowerment.

In the late 1800s William Hesketh Lever built Port Sunlight Village to house his soap factory workers. The aim of the housing was to provide a safe, secure and healthy environment to live in, by ensuring that people had access to clean water and improved sanitation. Lever claimed that Port Sunlight Village was an exercise in engaging people in profit sharing. Whilst this benevolent approach to his employees was admirable, it is interesting to note that he is quoted as saying that he invested in the village rather than distributing profits amongst his workers, as he feared they would spend it on "bottles of whisky, bags of sweets, or fat geese at Christmas."

Another forward thinking employer was the Cadbury family, who set up works committees as early as 1905. The remit of the committees was to consider working conditions, health, safety, education, training and the social life of the factory and its workers. In 1918, democratically elected works councils were set up, made up of equal numbers of management and worker representatives, who engaged in discussions and decisions about the workplace.

Both of these employers went on to build enormously successful and profitable organisations, selling products around the world. I am sure they also realised their philanthropy of empowering employees to lead healthier lives and engaging them in discussions about the workplace, led to significant benefits to their organisations. Investing in their employees' health and welfare meant reduced absenteeism and a fitter workforce. It also created loyalty that enabled them to build huge global brands. This shows how respect and consideration for people, along with Engaging and Empowering them to do the same for themselves and others is not just a 'hippy' ideal – it can be very good for business.

Another example of effective engagement is the 'Hawthorne Effect' research mentioned in Chapter 3. This research showed that involving people in discussions and decisions about the factory and its lighting led to improvements in productivity. It was not the change to the environment that led to the improvement; it was due to the engagement created by involving employees in the changes.

MODERN DAY MOTIVATION

The concepts of Engagement and Empowerment have continued to evolve and develop. Today many writers on people and motivation cite Engagement and Empowerment as fundamental elements that drive successful teams. Daniel Pink, in his book 'Drive: The surprising truth about what motivates us' (2011), speculates on changes to motivation since the early days of man, through Victorian times and up to the present day.

Pink defines different levels of motivation. As basic hunter-gatherers we were fulfilling Motivation 1.0, the basic instinct to survive. Subsequently we evolved from self-sufficiency living off the land, to working in factories and a worldwide shift to manufacturing. He cites this more organised survival as having led to 'carrot and stick' motivation, what he calls Motivation 2.0. Pink argues that a major problem for the world is that we are stuck at Motivation 2.0.

Some organisations think they are taking a radical approach to motivation by relaxing their dress code or providing rest areas with pool tables and a slide, but Pink calls this Motivation 2.1. He advocates embracing Motivation 3.0, which he describes as focusing on how we organise through our behaviours, which are driven more by intrinsic desires than extrinsic ones.

He points to how, as human beings, we have innate curiosity and drive that influence our behaviours. Intrinsic drives have taken us from cave dwelling hunters to being inventors and pioneers that have put human beings on the moon. This links to the 'Hierarchy of Needs' theory discussed in Chapter 4, which suggests we have a need to develop skills to become what we believe we are capable of, so that we are self fulfilled. It is these intrinsic drives that influence our motivation and behaviour in the workplace, and therefore how we perform.

When radical ideas are first raised they will often be dismissed as crazy and impossible to achieve. Yet the intrinsic drive within people, even when faced with what appear to be insurmountable odds, makes the seemingly impossible possible. As human beings we are constantly defying science, logic, common sense and our own personal safety. As a manager of people there will be times when you will marvel and despair at the behaviour of employees for just these reasons!

In his book, Pink cites examples of organisations that have seen success with novel approaches that encompass Motivation 3.0 and thus employees' intrinsic motivation. Some of these examples include doing away with rigid rules and structures for working times and reporting lines. Within minimal parameters that set output requirements, employees are fully empowered to make decisions impacting on how and when they work, which has led to significant business success.

Employees are not the poorly educated masses of Victorian times. They are responsible for making decisions about their own lives and can make informed choices about what they do and where they work. That includes choosing to work in a safe environment for someone who is supportive and motivating, where they know what to do, are able to get on with it, and can share their thoughts on how things can be improved.

Despite what naysayers may predict, the removal of rigid controls and letting people make their own decisions has not resulted in total anarchy or employees frittering away their earnings on "fat geese at Christmas".

If we want to harness the potential of Motivation 3.0 we need to have a working environment that does not set and expect people to follow rigid rules and structures. One problem in doing this is that our early experiences which establish our values and approaches to work are set within rigid rules and structures as defined at school. The nature of any education system is such that it adheres to a fixed timetable and curriculum. In our formative years we are regularly told what we have to do and when we have to do it. Even at College or University, though people choose to be there, they still have to adhere to a set timetable for lectures and examinations.

The challenge for employers is to avoid establishing a working environment where managers act as teachers with employees expecting their working lives to be mapped out for them. This can be achieved by harnessing intrinsic drives to develop an effective working environment that encourages positive behaviours through Engagement and Empowerment.

Employees do not need to be constantly watched to make sure that they work. However, as individuals, employees will sit on a spectrum of intrinsic motivation. Unfortunately, some people will apply their intrinsic drive into actually trying to avoid work. Others will have a surfeit so that you find yourself managing their over enthusiasm. The common denominator with employees is that you need to set and monitor their individual tasks and targets. However, the regularity with which you do so will need to be tailored to each employee. The way to do this is through regular one to one communication.

Having an awareness of intrinsic motivation and the positive results that can be achieved through Engaging and Empowering people will help you to effectively manage the individuals in your teams. However, don't slavishly copy the radical methods of work planning used by other organisations. Think about how you can engage the intrinsic potential of everyone in a way that is best suited to your team and organisation.

HEALTHY COMPETITION

Engagement and Empowerment should not focus purely on what an individual can do for themselves or their team. The overall aim of Engagement and Empowerment is to achieve the organisation's goals and we should all be on the same side in trying to achieve them.

This necessitates not unwittingly setting groups into competition against each other in a negative way. It can be good to create some internal competition and pit department against department in a quiz or in achieving separate team targets. Where it becomes potentially damaging is when it creates 'tribalism' and when 'all for one and one for all' turns teams into bitter rivals. As with team based incentives illustrated in Chapter 7, there is the potential for rivalries to become destructive to individuals, and the whole organisation, if people struggle to cooperate effectively with their colleagues.

SIZE MATTERS

Another area to consider in respect of Engaging and Empowering is team size. Managers need to be aware that smaller factions may split out of larger groups, which can lead to informal teams within departments setting themselves against each other. Commentators on team size have differing opinions about the optimum size of a group. For some it is 8 to 12, while others argue it is 4 to 7. There is no definitive number, but there is some agreement that increasing numbers eventually leads to reduced effectiveness. Writers on team size often point to the 'Ringelmann Effect' named after Maximilian Ringelmann (1913), a French agricultural engineer born in 1861. To study the effect of group numbers, Ringelmann asked people to pull a rope and gradually increased the numbers pulling on it. He discovered that the more people who pulled on the rope, the less effort each individual contributed.

The 'perfect' group size will vary according to the team members, the manager and nature of the work being carried out. If your team is growing in number, then consider whether you might encounter the 'Ringelmann Effect'.

Whatever the group size, the team targets and internal rivalries, it is down to you as the boss to ensure that your teams remain collaborative and are working to achieve the organisation's overall goals. Regularly remind them that you are all on the same side, and engage them in discussions about achieving the organisation's overarching goals. To avoid teams developing internal rivalries arrange regular 'all team' meetings and socials events that can break down barriers and cultivate a cohesive organisation.

I have seen this work well for a client who takes all employees off site for two full days every three months to discuss and plan the organisation's strategy. Various activities over the two days are structured to cover business planning as well as learning about aspects of team behaviour, and social events. Different sessions involve groups working within their regular teams, and mixing people from different teams. This conscious approach to team building enables individuals and teams to develop wider and stronger lines of communications that results in a cohesive organisation.

LET'S TALK

It is important to recognise and follow the values and behaviour associated with Engagement and Empowerment. Values that have a positive effect on people and teams include being fair, ethical, respectful and inclusive. The behaviour includes listening, delegating and open communication.

Regular one to one communication is a thread common to many areas of People Management discussed in this book. There is no set template for frequency or duration but effective Engagement and Empowerment requires more than just asking questions of an employee once or twice a year during an appraisal. It should include a regular 'health check' asking what people are doing, how they are doing it, discussing whether targets are being achieved, and if they are aware of the overall goals of the team and the whole organisation? (See Chapter 5 for examples of 'health check' questions to ask.)

As the boss it is down to you to set targets and boundaries, and to regularly monitor both. You can also give permission for people to take on additional responsibility and increased levels of decision-making within discussed and agreed parameters.

Increased responsibility can include helping to develop the potential of other team members through the sharing of skills, knowledge and experience. A positive effect of this is that people become more confident and more likely to question unclear information and resolve problems quickly, with minimal intervention from you. But be aware that you need to distinguish between those who raise questions in a constructive manner, and those that do so just to be disruptive.

You can also implement practices and policies that encourage your people and teams to interact, including employee lunches, events and meetings. You can engage your whole team by carrying out an employee survey. However, it is essential that if you ask people their opinions, you must be seen to take action. If you ask for input then be prepared to listen and carefully consider, debate and respond, or you will soon lose all credibility and people will not bother to contribute.

Don't just ask if people want to wear jeans to work, or what flavour crisps they want in the vending machine. Ask for their input and opinions on the values, goals, outputs and working conditions of the organisation.

These approaches will lead to more effective team working, ensure higher levels of satisfaction, reduce employee turnover, and improve productivity. Along with improved levels of decision-making amongst team members, it means that you will have more time to develop yourself and fulfil your role within the organisation.

THE FIVE KEY FACTORS – ENGAGEMENT AND EMPOWERMENT

The Five Key Factors embodied by managers I first described in Chapter 1 can be applied to your approach to Engagement and Empowerment:

1. Enthusiasm
For exploring ways of developing the team and giving opportunities for individuals to grow and take on more responsibility. This includes recognising that as a boss a vital aspect of your role is to engage and empower all team members because you want to see people grow and achieve.

2. Open Communication
As well as regular one to one's with individuals; a fundamental aspect of effective Engagement and Empowerment is to ensure that you have regular open communication with teams and the wider organisation. This will encourage the development of open communication between all team members.

3. A Head for Business and a Heart for People
Engaging and empowering people is not only good for the health and welfare of your team, it is also good for business. Treating people well and fairly will reap rewards in respect of increased performance and productivity.

4. Engaging and Empowering
Motivation is a fundamental part of managing people in order to achieve the desired performance of your organisation. This is accomplished by recognising that people are not there to be 'bossed about' and having in place a strategy and processes that encourage input from everyone and harnessing the intrinsic drive of people.

5. Listening and Learning
Regular one to ones form the basis of gathering and sharing information and ideas across the whole organisation that can help to drive the success of the organisation. This will enable you to develop yourself, your personal success and the effectiveness of the organisation.

SUMMARY – ENGAGEMENT AND EMPOWERMENT

Engagement and empowerment are not just good for people; they have been shown to be good for business as they can lead to improved performance, increased productivity and achieving organisational goals.

Your Engagement and Empowerment strategy should include the following:

1. **Engage people by sharing information and involving them in decisions wherever possible.**

2. **Empower people with knowledge, responsibility and support. Delegate within agreed parameters but don't abdicate responsibility to identify and resolve problems.**

3. **Successful motivation is achieved through communication with people to identify and satisfy their intrinsic drives.**

4. **Effective communication with individuals and between teams is an essential part of Engagement and Empowerment.**

5. **As the boss, make sure you employ the Five Key Factors identified in Chapter 1.**

In Chapter 9 we look at how a proactive approach to developing people can enhance the performance of you, your teams and your organisation.

CHAPTER NINE

PEOPLE DEVELOPMENT

If you've been sequentially working through this book you'll have realised the inescapable reality that People Management doesn't end after recruitment.

If you sit back and hope that the people you recruit will perform perfectly and your organisation will prosper, you will be disappointed. This nirvana doesn't happen. It is essential that you manage the continuous development of individuals, teams and yourself. This includes developing the knowledge, skills and experience of both new recruits and current employees.

A proactive approach to developing your people is a key element of building a high performing team.

When I first started out in the world of People Management, employee development was called Training. More recently a range of titles have come into use including 'talent management'. I prefer to use People Development as this accurately describes the intention and purpose of what happens after someone is appointed or promoted into a job. It includes skills training and learning achieved via courses or instruction and covers personal development through coaching, mentoring or self-learning.

People Development applies to all the members of your team, and includes people with little ambition beyond doing the same job until retirement, as well as high flyers. Changes to the world of work through continuing advancements in technology mean that even the non high flyer will at some point have to learn something different, even if it is just a new software version.

People develop knowledge, skills and experience from the day that you appoint them and it continues throughout their employment. The work that people do will also develop as external factors change such as those illustrated with the Open Systems Theory in Chapter 4.

Encouraging an environment of People Development can help your organisation to meet its evolving needs for performance and delivery as well as self-fulfilling the people in it. People who develop in a role can also use their new skills, knowledge and experience to help others.

A GOOD PLACE TO START: TAKING CARE OF THE BASICS

You may have worked for, or be working in, an organisation that has someone who is responsible for People Development. However, thinking that it can be left to your 'Training Manager' or a 'Talent Management' department, and that it doesn't have to feature in your role as a boss is a mistake.

A conscious approach to engaging everyone in People Development can ensure you have a team that is doing what you need it to do, in a way that is efficient and effective for all concerned.

It is at this point that you may be hoping for detailed instructions to follow, but as with most aspects of People Management there is no set way of developing people. It will differ from person to person, and you as the boss will also be a factor. Whilst there is no magic formula for People Development, there are some basic dos and don'ts:

1. **Don't just rely on holding an appraisal meeting once or twice a year.**

2. **Don't apply it just to the employees who want to take on more tasks and responsibilities, or who are eager for training or promotion.**

3. **Don't think it is just about sending people on training courses.**

4. **Do recognise that developing all the people in your team is part of the day-to-day activities of being the boss.**

5. **Do acknowledge that people will have different reasons for working and different ambitions in respect of their life and career. As a result they will have different personal development needs.**

6. **Do remember that an approach that works for one person isn't guaranteed to work for another.**

Whilst not an exact science, People Development is not complicated. Despite this I am surprised how often managers fail to cover the basics at the expense of performance and employee turnover.

One of these basics is that People Development starts from the first day that a person joins your team. The first day is crucial in establishing the employment relationship you have with them, and can make all the difference in defining initial impressions.

Depending on how confident someone is, their first day can range from a terrifying experience to a walk in the park. For everyone, the aim should be for them to experience a well thought out and structured first day. The induction plan is not the sole responsibility of the training department. As the boss, make sure you are involved and ensure you are a part of their first day and week. It is also a good idea to include members from the team the new employee will be working with. They are likely to have suggestions based on good or bad induction experiences they may have had, or volunteer to help and be a 'buddy'.

Induction is more than just filling in forms, issuing tools and uniforms, or showing someone the facilities. It is an early opportunity to begin the process of team building. This doesn't require taking everyone out for a day to tackle an assault course. It is about ensuring that plenty of time is allowed for relaxed introductions between the people who will be working together.

Don't put new starters under pressure from the outset by truncating the induction because there is a backlog of work that needs to be tackled. If you start them in a stressful environment their first impressions will be negative, and reduce the likelihood of them becoming a long-term employee. Also, just because you have recruited someone you consider to be the right person, with the right skills and personality, don't assume that from their first day they will know exactly what you want them to do, and the way that you want them to do it.

In my experience, effective induction is not just about the first day; it is about the whole of the first week. I have seen numerous examples where someone has not returned after their first day and just as many when they don't return after their first week. Common reasons given include; that they were just left to get on with an unfamiliar job, or were not fully introduced to or made to feel part of the team.

There is no established template for the perfect induction programme. As a minimum and as a good place to start, induction should be developed to ensure that the physiological, security and social needs are covered as described by Maslow (see Chapter 4).

The physiological basics include making sure someone knows how they are going to be paid, where they can go for food or drink and where the essential facilities are. The security basics include health and safety training, particularly if the job has inherent risks.

The area that tends to be missed is the social need for friendship and belonging to a group. This can be covered by ensuring that plenty of time is allocated during the induction to meet with colleagues. It also helps if they are allocated a mentor from within the team, (not the boss), that they can go to with questions or concerns.

I have also found it useful to have a meeting with the new person at the end of their first day, and at the end of their first week. As with any meeting, the quality comes not only from spending time with someone, but from the questions you ask and what you do as a result of the answers. It is an opportunity to find out if the recruit has any concerns that may prevent them coming back tomorrow, or the following week. It is also a good opportunity for both of you to discuss ideas and thoughts about any training and development that may help them settle in.

It is also useful to have similar meetings with team members they are working with to identify any potential issues. Early intervention can prevent minor issues developing into bigger problems.

IT'S GOOD TO TALK

Many issues that manifest as poor performance can arise from a lack of People Development. Failure to quickly identify and tackle problems someone has in understanding how to do a job can lead to a situation that becomes more difficult to resolve.

As I mentioned earlier on in this chapter, People Development is part of the day-to-day activities of being the boss, and is not difficult if you are having regular meetings with your employees at which their development needs are discussed. The time you take to have short, regular meetings is time invested in the overall running of your team and organisation. If you think that you either don't have time, or don't need to have these meetings because things seem to be running well, you risk facing issues that could become bigger and more time consuming.

The term 'regular' applied to these meetings varies depending on the individual and the circumstances involved. They might be daily for people new to a role but much less frequent for others. Regular does not mean only once or twice a year during appraisal or performance reviews.

Whilst the timing of the meetings may differ, one thing that should be consistent is the quality of the questions you ask. You don't need to have a long list and work your way through all of them at each meeting. Adapt the conversation to the current situation. Subject areas to cover can include; what coaching support they may need from you, if they feel they need any skills or personal development training, or if they are interested in taking on different tasks or responsibilities. These are particularly important if you are discussing changing what someone is asked to deliver, or are setting them new objectives.

Identifying personal development needs is the first stage, but just as important, is to identify and deliver the most appropriate solution. This is not just about sending people on a training course, but can include shadowing, mentoring and e-learning. Other critical factors to cover are; what the outcome will be, regularly monitoring progress, and ensuring you are delivering the aspects of their development you have agreed to help with.

HERE WE GO AGAIN ...

So we come to the thorny matter of yearly or twice yearly reviews. These are usually called appraisals or performance reviews and, in my experience, are often used in organisations as the only tool for identifying Personal Development needs. Whilst what it is called may vary in organisations, the process usually follows the same format. It is a specific meeting held once or twice a year, during which a line manager meets with an employee to review their performance objectives as well as their training and development needs. Appraisal meetings often follow a set process of preparation, meeting format and follow up that requires completion of various forms.

In my experience the mention of appraisals can produce a gamut of responses from adoration, through ambivalence to abhorrence (but adoration is in the minority!).

The responses are usually governed by the quality of the process. Negative factors can include:

- **An over reliance on paperwork that asks exam type questions which seem to require essay answers.**
- **The process is imposed from on high.**
- **Agreed actions are not followed up.**
- **The process stays the same and each meeting becomes a repetition of the last.**
- **It is used to bring up issues that are a surprise to the employee.**

The common denominators where appraisals are seen positively include:

- **Paperwork is used as a guide and it is not compulsory to fill in lots of boxes or information.**
- **The focus is on personal development needs and how these can be met.**

- Regular follow up meetings happen after the 'main' meeting which leads to agreed personal development needs being met.

- The emphasis is on the individual to also take responsibility for their personal development, and not just the manager dictating to the employee how they want them to develop.

When working with clients I am often asked if I have an appraisal process they can copy and 'get their managers to use' with their employees. When asked why they feel they need to have an appraisal process, answers have included "that's what other companies do" and "because we had one in my last organisation". I am very rarely told that they want to use it as part of an approach to an overall strategy of People Development.

When I probe into why an organisation wants to introduce an appraisal process, it often highlights a problem that needs resolving with a different approach such as performance management. Performance and behavioural issues should be tackled separately as they arise and should not be stored up for an appraisal meeting (see Chapter 10).

What I would like to hear is that they want to conduct appraisals to identify and meet the individual development needs of their employees and thereby drive their organisation forward.

It is not compulsory to have an appraisal process and one shouldn't be introduced just because other organisations do, or use it to confront people with issues.

Many organisations fall into the trap of treating an appraisal process as a product that can be bought 'off the shelf'. Numerous web-based companies offer a range of template forms to buy or subscribe to. There are also companies that sell IT based Performance Management systems, offering automation for the whole process. Resist the temptation to just buy off the shelf products or recycle forms you have collected from a past employer. Whilst this may be tempting as a quick fix, it will not pay dividends in the long term. Your organisation is unique and will benefit more from a bespoke process that has been developed with input from your team.

Some appraisals are structured so that the employee can receive a pay increase or bonus payment if they achieve set targets or objectives. Do not presume that doing this automatically leads to increased productivity or performance. There is no foolproof appraisal process linked to a pay increase or bonus that will guarantee significantly increased outputs or performance.

If you have or are considering developing appraisals linked to salary increases or bonus payments, you need to think very carefully about the process and the additional work and challenges that it can create (see Chapter 7).

A few large organisations have identified some benefits of an integrated and robust competence based appraisal process linked to pay progression. However, they have the resources, money and infrastructure to set up, continually monitor, and manage it.

Many organisations that have linked pay to appraisals encounter problems such as escalating costs, heavy demands on manager's time to implement and carry out the process, problems of assessment, employee resistance and equal opportunities considerations.

On top of these issues are the inevitable debates, negotiation, and disputes that you will face with people dissatisfied with how their performance is measured and what increase or bonus they receive.

From my experience I would not recommend having an appraisal process linked to pay, the problems outweigh the potential benefits.

It may be that your organisation dictates that an ineffective review process remains in place, and you are not able to change it. In this case, consider other factors to use as motivators when planning objectives and identifying training and development needs for your team (see Job Enrichment). Also, the process doesn't prevent you from having regular one to one meetings with your team to discuss their ongoing development needs outside of the set procedures.

ASK THE PEOPLE

If you want to introduce or update an appraisal process as part of a wider People Development strategy, (whether or not it is linked to pay increases or bonus payments) start by looking at the wealth of information available online. A common theme will be that an essential part of developing any process is gathering input from the employees and managers who are actually going to be using it. They are fundamental to the success of an appraisal process. It is also important that it reflects the culture and values of your organisation.

One problem evident in many organisations is that writing up appraisal forms becomes a time consuming chore for line managers. As an alternative I have developed processes for clients where it is the employee who is responsible for writing up brief notes from the meeting. In some instances it is also down to the employee to identify and approach their own mentor, or present a case for a course they want to go on. As a result these tasks are more likely to be done when it is one of a few things on the employee's 'to do' list rather than being one of many on the line manager's list. It is also more likely to be done if the employee is keen to do it, rather than being something that the manager dictates that they should do.

However, you don't want people to think that you are not interested in helping them to develop. Encouraging them to 'fend for themselves' needs to be balanced with being involved in supporting them, checking their progress and reinforcing that you are there to help. Your support can come in the form of coaching, suggesting mentors, pointing them to courses and learning opportunities, suggesting books to read, or looking out for other sources of information, and can be part of regular one to one meetings.

A risk in introducing an appraisal process is that it can result in managers waiting for the meetings before talking to their teams about development. People Development needs to be a year round activity.

The most effective processes I have seen specify that regular one to one meetings continue to take place after the 'main' appraisal meeting to progress objectives and development. This gives the opportunity to check if agreed actions are being delivered. Remember that as the line manager, you and the process will lose credibility if you fail to deliver on agreed actions.

PEOPLE DEVELOPMENT ALTERNATIVES

Traditional appraisal processes concentrate on developing increasing knowledge and skills focused on the job or organisation's needs. However, some organisations are moving to a policy of allowing employees to use a percentage of their work time to volunteer or develop non-work related skills. In Google it was known as 20% Time, and it led to employees developing and improving the organisation's products.

Many organisations have found that they are more likely to retain employees if their creativity is encouraged rather than restricted. The added advantage is the organisation benefits from the improved knowledge and skills people develop through their drive to learn and do more. Encouraging personal development through other routes, either directly linked to work or not, could be beneficial to your organisation.

There are many excellent sources of information available about the theory and practice of training and development, showing how different approaches work for different people. If you employ people, I urge you to develop yourself by making use of these freely available resources.

JOB ENRICHMENT

Research shows that one way to meet People Development needs is via job enrichment, which in turn leads to improved performance. An early study was conducted by a clinical psychologist called Frederick Herzberg (1959) who is seen by many as the pioneer of job enrichment. Through research into motivation at work, he developed a model called the Motivator-Hygiene Theory (also known as the Two factor theory) of job satisfaction. According to his theory people are influenced by two sets of factors, hygiene factors and positive motivators.

He identified the following items in each category:

Hygiene Factors

Pay, benefits, relationship with subordinates and supervisors, working conditions, supervision style, status, job security and personal life.

Positive Motivators

Type of work, challenge/achievement, promotion prospects/ advancement, responsibility and recognition/esteem.

Herzberg's work established that:

- Whilst hygiene factors will not motivate employees, if there is a problem with them then they could be a demotivating factor. For example, a hygiene factor can include working conditions, such as a clean office. If the office is dirty, it can lead to complaints and demotivation but once the office is cleaned up, then the tidy environment does not in itself lead to greater motivation.

- Whilst the absence of positive motivational factors will not necessarily lower motivation, they can be responsible for increasing motivation. For example, a positive motivational factor can include promotion prospects. The lack of promotion prospects in an organisation does not have the effect of actively lowering motivation, but if they are introduced it can lead to enhanced motivation.

Note that no factor appears in both lists. A common mistake is to confuse items between the lists, particularly pay. Pay is a hygiene factor so if pay is an issue to the employee, it can be demotivating. However, if pay is not an issue to the employee then it is not in itself a positive motivator. The type of work an employee does and their promotion prospects have the capacity to be a more positive motivator than pay.

It is important to remember that problems with 'hygiene' factors need to be addressed to avoid demotivation, but that the actual motivators that can lead to enhanced performance are actions concerning achievement, advancement and development.

Job enrichment can be identified within the regular one to ones as mentioned earlier in this chapter. It doesn't have to be saved for appraisal time.

DEVELOPMENT FOR EVERYONE

I have encountered bosses who will not pay to train employees for fear it will equip them with skills that would encourage them to work elsewhere. This is shortsighted and wrong. If the employee is keen to learn and develop, and they are not encouraged to do so, they will seek opportunities elsewhere anyway. Not withstanding the lost opportunity to have benefited from the employee's increased contribution to your organisation, you will also lose time and money in having to replace them. An increase in performance from training and development can lead to an increase in productivity that will outweigh the cost. So viewing the 'bigger picture', training can actually represent an increase in income well in excess of the cost.

For smaller organisations without a substantial training budget or obvious lines of promotion, the challenge can be to keep ambitious high flyers. In this instance Herzberg's research into job enrichment, as discussed above, can help. Enriching and developing a job is not about making a job larger by getting an employee to do more of the same. Development is giving them more meaningful tasks, coaching them in new skills, and allowing them more autonomy for decision-making.

Don't fall into the trap of thinking that it is just the high flyers that want to be, or should be, developed. You may have employees who don't have lofty ambitions, but you still want them to work reliably and deliver a good standard of work. Like the high flyer, the person who just wants to come to work to do the same job day in day out will still need to develop. Software upgrades, a new piece of equipment, or a new product or service will all necessitate developing through additional knowledge or skills.

Do not assume that employees are resistant to change. I have seen many instances where people have been unfairly 'written off' by others. Coaching tailored to the individual that shows them what needs to change and why, how it will impact on them, and the support they will be given, will help them to overcome fears or resistance.

Don't forget, that you need to keep developing yourself. Continuing to learn or improve your technical and People Management skills will help you become alert to opportunities to develop and enhance the performance of your team and organisation.

As a manager you are also a coach or mentor, and your team will look to you for support through your knowledge and experience. If you are in an organisation with an ineffective boss and a misfiring appraisal process, you can still drive your own personal development through self-learning. Advancing your knowledge and skills can give you a significant business advantage. A coach or mentor can help you to develop yourself, your organisation and the people you employ. You and your team's People Development should not be seen as a luxury or an additional time or financial cost, it is a sound business investment.

AN ACTIVE APPROACH

If you are managing a team People Development should be part of your day-to-day activities. Research by Maslow (see Chapter 4) illustrates that people need to develop through the hierarchy of needs, not only to meet their physiological, safety and social needs, but to also develop self-esteem. This is the need to develop skills to enable us to achieve what we feel is our full potential.

Leaving people to just get on with it, or limiting conversations to an appraisal meeting once or twice a year may get the job done, but opportunities to drive greater performance are being missed. There is also the risk of higher turnover and performance issues that can negatively impact on productivity. An active approach to developing people can enhance the skills and morale of all of the members of your team.

THE FIVE KEY FACTORS – PEOPLE DEVELOPMENT

The Five Key Factors embodied by managers I first described in Chapter 1 can be applied to your approach to People Development:

1. Enthusiasm

To ensure that People Development is advocated, identified and met for everyone in your team and for yourself.

2. Open Communication

Holding regular one to one discussions and being open about performance needs and opportunities for personal development, is key to building a high performing team.

3. A Head for Business and a Heart for People

Training and development is not an indulgence or an unnecessary expense – it is good for business. The additional skills employees build can then be used to develop others in the organisation, to continue a cycle of growing effective performance leading to increased productivity.

4. Engaging and Empowering

Engaging with people to discuss and develop ways to enrich their jobs and to offer individual development will lead to increased self esteem, personal satisfaction, and improved productivity and performance. This applies to all employees and will empower them to develop themselves, and work with you to meet an identified need.

5. Listening and Learning

Talk to your team and listen to what development needs they have. Learn about and keep abreast of different ways to meet those needs, which will mean that you are continuously developing your understanding and awareness of People Development.

SUMMARY – PEOPLE DEVELOPMENT

A conscious approach to People Development through having regular conversations with your team, which cover personal development, is time and cost effective and will help you identify and meet needs that can raise performance.

A successful approach to People Development includes ensuring that:

1. **Opportunities for development are available to everyone.**

2. **Discussions over personal development are ongoing rather than just talked about once or twice a year.**

3.**If you have an appraisal process, engage employees in developing an approach that works and benefits them, and your organisation.**

4. **Meeting development needs is not just limited to sending people on a training course.**

5.**As the boss, make sure you are following the Five Key Factors with respect to the development of your team and yourself.**

In Chapter 10 we look at the challenges of managing the performance of individuals and teams, including what you can do to avoid small problems becoming bigger ones.

CHAPTER TEN

PERFORMANCE MANAGEMENT

If you manage people, a fundamental requirement of your job is to maximise their performance. The majority of the people you manage will deliver what is expected of them and will do a good job.

I would like to say that Performance Management only ever involves positive aspects of improving and developing your team via People Development (see Chapter 9), but an inescapable aspect of employing people is that you will have to deal with difficult situations impacting negatively on performance.

Performance Management is about ensuring the people in your team are carrying out the work you need them to do, by the required timescales and to the prescribed standard. It involves setting individual, team and organisation goal focused tasks and subsequently ensuring they are achieved. This will mean tackling problems that get in the way of achieving those tasks and targets.

Successful managers I have worked with want to build a successful organisation where people enjoy being at work. In an ideal world employees come to work as planned, carry out tasks efficiently and everyone in the team gets along. As we don't live in an ideal world you will find that Performance Management will also include discussions about problems between employees, challenging unacceptable performance and behaviours, and dealing with disciplinary and grievance matters. As the boss you will need to build trust by dealing with people problems in a consistent and fair way.

An additional challenge with Performance Management is that people are influenced by conditions outside of the workplace. As discussed in Chapter 4, Open Systems Theory reminds us that external environmental factors will affect your employees, and these are likely to be beyond your control.

A conscious and consistent approach to Performance Management will help you to develop a high performing team. Creating conditions that maximise performance is also likely to minimise other workplace problems.

A GOOD PLACE TO START: KEEP IT SIMPLE

Performance Management is not complicated. In simple terms for your team it means they need to:

- **Know what they have to do, the targets they have to achieve and the timescales involved.**

- **Be made aware of required standards of performance and behaviour when at work.**

- **Have or develop the skills to do the work you want them to do.**

- **Understand the organisation goals, and the part they have to play in achieving them.**

Your Performance Management tasks will include:

- **Giving clear direction and coaching to all of the members of your team. This includes pointing out the good and the less good of what they are doing.**

- **Creating an environment of effective team support.**

- **Ensuring people are given the resources, tools, coaching and training necessary to do their job. The coaching includes ensuring they understand their freedom to make decisions and the limits of their authority.**

- **That as well as communicating (and following) the standards for performance and behaviour that are required of your team, you take prompt, consistent and even handed action when they are not being met.**

When developing an approach to Performance Management, a good place to start is ensuring you have the right number of people, with the right level of ability, and to provide them with the tools, training and personal development (see Chapter 9), they need to carry out their jobs.

The output of your organisation can be damaged by a lack of resources. The reasons can include not providing the right tools, absenteeism, or insufficient people. In respect of employee numbers, it is a balance between keeping costs under control and having enough people to do the work. The significant risk from too high a workload due to a lack of resources is stress, which results in time off work that compounds the problem. It also means there is no energy or goodwill left for times when there is an emergency or a surge in work.

DOING IT FOR THE TEAM

People Management is not just about individuals doing whatever is necessary to ensure they achieve their own targets. The overall performance of the team can be negatively impacted if individuals only focus on what they do and not how it impacts on others in the organisation. You can set standards of performance that encompass how people work together, who works with whom, and how, along with overall targets for the team.

It would be naïve to expect that everyone will always get on and that team members won't come into conflict with each other at some point. There are many theories about the way groups work together and develop. One of the better known is Bruce Tuckman (1965) and his 'Forming – Storming – Norming – Performing' model of group development. He stated that it is necessary for teams to go through the four phases of the model so that it can deal with challenges, solve problems and deliver results. It should be noted that teams go though these stages again each time someone joins or leaves the team.

In the 'storming' stage, there is often conflict as ideas compete to be accepted and are challenged by questioning. Through this process team members learn about each other, work out how to function together and decide who does what.

Tuckman argues that the 'storming' stage is necessary for the growth of a team. If team members avoid difficult issues or always agree with each other, then there is a potential for paralysis by politeness. Challenging thoughts and approaches can push boundaries and test the robustness of ideas resulting in team growth.

Many theories of group behaviour at work agree that conflict, including testing out new ways of doing things and pushing boundaries, is a necessary part of developing a high performing team. This can lead to creative conflict that enables the team to reach a better outcome. The challenge is ensuring that the conflict remains at the lower end of the spectrum, and is based on an approach of mutual support and constructive criticism, rather than enmity and aggression.

As a manager you must encourage a safe environment where constructive criticism is acceptable. You must also take action to ensure that matters do not descend into anarchy and that conflict is resolved. If the group cannot move beyond 'storming' via conflict resolution to 'norming', the risk is that it will get stuck and damage productivity. You will need to set boundaries and standards of behaviour that will include allowing your own thoughts and ideas to be critiqued. You also need to be aware that some people are conflict averse and will need more support with this approach, as they will still have a valuable contribution to make.

You must also be tolerant, firm, fair and directive in the absence of consensus. Agreeing to disagree is an acceptable outcome to a conflict situation. In order to avoid the group becoming stuck, you may have to act as mediator or a judge. You must also be prepared to make decisions that move the team on, which may be unpopular with one or more of its members. This will also include challenging unacceptable performance or behaviours, particularly if they are negatively impacting on other team members.

A proactive approach to Performance Management will acknowledge the potential for conflict. It will also set the standards of behaviour as a framework to avoid matters becoming personal. People don't have to be best friends with everyone but they do have to act respectfully and professionally toward each other at all times.

NIPPING IT IN THE BUD

The behaviour of individuals can have a significant impact on their colleagues. Behaviour such as absence, bullying, gossiping, being abrupt, rude or over critical will have a negative effect on workplace morale and can make coming to work an unpleasant experience. This can lead to an increase in absenteeism and a decrease in productivity.

Whether employees complain to you directly, you observe issues, or others mention concerns, there is an expectation that as the manager you will resolve the problem. Whilst you are not responsible for solving all of the issues in people's lives, failure to tackle those at work will damage your reputation and your ability to motivate your team. It will also cost you time and money in dealing with the fallout from ignored issues, to the detriment of your own performance.

Early intervention is key to tackling performance issues. Having an environment with regular and open communication will help to facilitate this. I appreciate that, even with regular communication, initiating conversations about problems can be difficult. It can be hard to deal with employees who are unhappy, angry, under performing, regularly absent, are being unpleasant to each other, or have lied or stolen.

It is an understandable aspect of human nature to want to avoid conflict and things we find difficult or unpleasant to deal with. Avoiding the issue is an option, but not one I recommend. From experience I have seen that the problem doesn't go away, and inevitably the issue becomes bigger and more difficult to resolve, with greater fallout. This fallout can consume even more of your time and the issue will become more difficult to deal with.

Human nature may also mean we avoid what seems to be a minor issue between two people. We may even speculate that it could be made worse if we get involved. This is an excuse and not a reason to avoid having a conversation with the people concerned. An informal discussion with both parties may resolve the issue or uncover others that need to be addressed. In my experience, it is very unlikely to make things worse, and quite often it comes as a relief to those directly and indirectly involved.

Before talking to people about your concerns over their performance or behaviour, gather objective evidence in the form of examples that you can discuss with them. Doing this will also enable you to check the claims of the complainants to assess that they are reasonable and not unfairly placing blame where it is unwarranted. If the person the complaint is about denies the issue or demands evidence, you are then well placed to respond. This will help if you are dealing with someone who refuses to see that it is their behaviour that is the underlying factor in a team's problems. They may look to avoid accountability or culpability, and apply blame elsewhere or claim to be the victim. This is more difficult to do in the face of objective evidence about their behaviour.

Once you have gathered and checked the facts, you are then in a position to discuss the matter. At the meeting, focus on discussing the person's actions rather than their personality, as this is emotive and likely to trigger a defensive response. Provide examples of a person's approach to work, or to others, rather than their 'attitude'.

Where possible have examples ready of their good performance or behaviour to reinforce the standards you are aiming for them to achieve.

In the meeting discuss and agree what the ongoing standards are, any targets to achieve these, and timescales for completion and review. As part of this agreed Performance Management programme you will also have to offer support, ensure any development needs are met and monitor their ongoing performance. You must be clear about the potential consequences of failing to meet the required performance targets, or standards of behaviour.

PREVENTION IS BETTER THAN CURE

The consequences of poor Performance Management include a negative impact on morale. This will damage performance and it will cost you time, money and stress. These problems can be minimised if you have a proactive Performance Management strategy. The good news is that the strategy is no more complicated than having regular, good quality conversations with your team, fulfilling what you have personally agreed to do, and tackling issues early. There is no exact definition of what 'regular' should be. The frequency will depend on the people involved (particularly if they work remotely).

As with developing people, successful Performance Management meetings are about the quality of the questions asked. As a minimum, discuss current workloads, targets, and standards. If these are not being achieved, the meeting should examine why and establish what problems need to be resolved, by whom and by when.

A tip when having meetings is to ensure that you ask 'open' questions that require more than one word answers and meaningful details. If you ask, "is everything going ok?" then you are more likely to hear the answer "yes", regardless of whether things are ok or not. I have seen situations where deadlines have been missed without apparent warning, despite regular performance meetings taking place; more often than not it is due to asking closed questions. Human nature means that people are often too proud, worried or resolutely over optimistic to raise the possibility that they may not be coping and instead give the answer they think the boss wants to hear.

Useful questions to ask that should prompt for more than one word answers include:

- **Where have you got to on this?**
- **What is left to be done before the deadline?**
- **What is getting in the way of completing this by the deadline?**
- **What can we or the team do to help?**

IT'S ALWAYS GOOD TO TALK

Regular meetings reinforce established objectives, but also give you an opportunity to prepare for potential changes.

It may seem obvious to say, but having regular conversations also helps to build rapport and trust with your employees. This has the benefit that they may raise issues that they would not have otherwise spoken up about.

One thing to avoid is only arranging to see an employee when there is a negative issue you want to raise with them. This can lead to people dreading the meetings and ultimately doing what they can to avoid them.

As with appraisals (see Chapter 9) if you have actions resulting from the meeting it is very important that you fulfil them, otherwise you and the meetings will lose creditability.

If a meeting highlights difficult issues then remember it is essential to tackle them as soon as possible.

Regular and open communication will minimise performance related problems. However, there is no guarantee you won't have to deal with issues more formally through a grievance or disciplinary process. This requires Performance Management that involves conciliation between parties, disciplinary sanctions and the use of performance improvement plans. If this happens, a firm, fair, prompt and consistent approach to dealing with the issue is key. It is also important to ensure you are following employment law and your own organisation's policies. Issues and procedures can be complex, and it is easy to make a bad situation worse, so I strongly advise that you seek expert advice and support.

If a grievance or disciplinary issue is managed promptly and professionally it is possible to rescue the situation and produce a positive outcome. It can also minimise the collateral damage from the ripple effect travelling through a team or organisation.

TIME TO GO

Regardless of all that you do to proactively manage the performance of team members, there may still come a time when you have to consider that the only option left is dismissal.

No dismissal is straightforward, but clear-cut reasons include gross misconduct, or repeated failure after a number of warnings to perform or behave as reasonably required. Where it is more difficult is when a role has changed, as a team or the organisation evolves, and an employee is unable to meet the new demands despite their own best efforts and support from the organisation.

It is not incumbent on the organisation, to 'find' an alternative role for the person. If you have the opportunity, and can afford to, this may be an option for an employee who has been loyal and worked hard for the organisation. However, consideration has to be given to the potential negative effect on the morale of the rest of the team if they feel that they are 'carrying' someone. The risk is heightened if the person has been 'side lined' because they have behaved or performed badly, and the organisation is avoiding dealing with the problem.

Deciding that the time has come to terminate a person's employment is a difficult decision to make, but you may have to do it. If you have tried all possible solutions to tackle the performance issue with the person concerned, have advised them of the potential consequences of a failure to improve, have given them time and offered appropriate support and personal development, then your conscience should be clear that you have exhausted all reasonable options.

At this point you need to think carefully about how and when to have that difficult conversation. Matters that need to be considered include the requirements of employment law, the rights of the employee and the potential impact on them, the rest of the team and the whole organisation. If you haven't already had a conversation with a People Management specialist, now is the time to do so. Getting this wrong can be time consuming, expensive and traumatic for everyone.

Time, thought and careful planning can help to ensure that this most difficult of situations is handled correctly, professionally and with dignity for all concerned.

THE FIVE KEY FACTORS – PERFORMANCE MANAGEMENT

The Five Key Factors embodied by managers I first described in Chapter 1 can be applied to your approach to Performance Management:

1. Enthusiasm

Successful managers have the drive to encourage input from their team as a means to reveal opportunities for increased performance. They actively manage positive conflict, tackle issues promptly and fairly and lead by example with their own behaviour and performance.

2. Open Communication

Effective bosses define clear standards for performance and behaviour, with open and constructive feedback when there are shortfalls and praise when they are achieved. They keep people informed, exercise appropriate discretion, and show they are acting on issues raised.

3. A Head for Business and a Heart for People

A heart for the people means giving poor performers the chance and time to improve through supported development. A head for business means taking the hard decisions where necessary for the overall interest of the wider organisation.

4. Engaging and Empowering

Engaging regularly with each team member ensures issues and concerns can be raised promptly and confidentially. Empowering people can mean problems are resolved at source, or that they know when to seek support in tackling issues.

5. Listening and Learning

Successful managers regularly talk and listen to every member of the team. This enables them to identify problems early and thereby minimise their impact. They also learn from their previous experiences and adapt their future behaviour accordingly.

SUMMARY – PERFORMANCE MANAGEMENT

Successful Performance Management of all team members is fundamental to your success as the boss. You don't need complicated processes or expensive equipment but you do need to follow the essentials:

1. **Ensure clear communication of the required tasks, standards and deadlines, and provide the resources and training to optimise performance not just for individuals but for teams too.**

2. **Don't avoid problems, establish the facts and deal with them promptly.**

3. **Encourage two-way communication with employees to enable problems to be avoided or identified early.**

4. **Seek professional advice with difficult performance issues particularly if it may lead to dismissal.**

5. **Applying the Five Key Factors of Performance Management will ensure effective performance that will develop people, teams and the success of your organisation.**

In the final part of this book, I summarise the fundamentals of People Management and how it is an ongoing and constantly evolving aspect of being an effective manager of people.

THIS IS NOT THE END

In this book I have highlighted what managing people really entails. I have also set out the building blocks required to produce and implement effective People Management strategies in order to create a high performing team.

Summarised below are the fundamentals of People Management that will make your life as a manager of people easier and less stressful.

An important aspect of all of the fundamentals is the need to regularly review and develop them to ensure they remain relevant, up to date and appropriate for your team and organisation.

PEOPLE MANAGEMENT NEEDS PEOPLE

People are essential to an organisation. You will only develop a high performing team if you start by finding, appointing and developing the right people.

I have worked with many clients and what stands out consistently with the successful ones is they understand that people are key to their success. Your unique team forms a significant part of your competitive advantage and provides the basis of a successful organisation.

Successful People Management is based on ethics, openness, respect, fairness, engagement, empowerment, training and development, fair pay and good working conditions.

The aim of a People Management strategy is to deliver sustainable performance whilst maintaining the wellbeing of individuals, teams and the whole organisation, thereby achieving desired goals. It is not a feel good 'hippy' credo – it is good for business. Research shows that People Management strategies lead to improved organisation performance.

From a home based business of two employees to an international conglomerate employing hundreds of thousands, whatever they make, build or sell and however they do it, employees are the common denominator and the fundamental People Management strategies are the same.

You can develop a People Management strategy that meets the particular needs of your organisation by following the fundamentals as set out in this book:

- **Effective recruitment that finds and appoints the best people.**

- **Pay and benefits that recognise and reward effective performance.**

- **Engagement and Empowerment that allow people to get on with doing what they do best.**

- **People Development that advocates, identifies and meets opportunities for everyone in your team, including yourself.**

- **Performance Management that tackles issues early and ensures the team are carrying out work to the required standard.**

PEOPLE CHANGE

Change is inevitable, cannot be prevented and should be viewed positively. Human beings will remain unpredictable and people will move in and out of your team. In addition, employment laws will change and work will evolve in response to the world economy.

As with your people, your People Management strategy won't remain static – it should evolve and develop. The same applies to you as the Boss. Keep your technical skills and knowledge updated, which includes your People Management skills.

Research in all People Management fields continues and will lead to new ideas and thinking. Be open-minded but don't jump on the bandwagon of every trend and fad. Evaluate potential changes against the particular needs of your organisation.

WHY PEOPLE MANAGEMENT?

Whatever your experience of People Management, don't expect to find a magic formula that makes you the perfect manager who never has to deal with people issues. I am sorry to disappoint you but there isn't any magic. Due to the unpredictability of humans, the only guarantee I can give is that there will be people problems to manage.

You may well ask what is the point of having a People Management strategy if it doesn't prevent employee issues occurring? The point is that having an effective strategy minimises problems and makes managing issues and people easier. It leads to improved performance that translates into increased profits.

In simple terms, People Management is an essential and ongoing core activity that has a positive impact on individual and organisation performance.

WHAT'S IN IT FOR ME?

Taking a proactive approach to People Management means fewer people issues, less stress and more free time for you. By all means take time to acknowledge and bask in the success of your team, but don't rest on your laurels. Remember that the lives of people and the environment your organisation operates in do not remain static.

Use this free time on tasks needed to identify and maximise ongoing development opportunities for your team, the organisation and yourself. This includes holding regular one to one meetings to discuss and find solutions for potential problems (even when all is going well) and identifying personal development needs.

Invest time in developing yourself by finding a mentor or building a support network that can help you and your organisation. This investment can lead to a continuous cycle of development and growth that will result in increased business for your organisation and more personal success for you.

THE FIVE KEY FACTORS

This book is a reference tool that will help you deal with problems and develop future plans for your team. Don't try to memorise everything in it, but do keep in mind the Five Key Factors demonstrated by successful managers that are discussed throughout this book:

1. Enthusiasm

Successful managers and teams have a collective sense of purpose and enthusiasm. They see change as a positive opportunity.

2. Open Communication

Successful managers see the benefit of being open and seeking feedback about an organisation's plans. They provide regular opportunities for everyone to give and receive honest feedback about their performance, work environment and the organisation.

3. A Head for Business and a Heart for People

Successful managers focus on achieving targets but acknowledge the most effective way to do this is by treating people with respect and building an ethical and fun working environment. They balance compassion with objectivity and take prompt, appropriate action to deal with unacceptable behaviour or performance.

4. Engaging and Empowering

Successful managers engage with and give everyone a voice. They encourage personal development for all. They acknowledge the benefits of empowering people to develop their experience, knowledge, personal and technical skills, and job responsibilities.

5. Listening and Learning

Only paying lip service to feedback is a lost opportunity to enhance performance, build a high performing team and develop a successful organisation. Successful managers listen to and learn from others, admit their mistakes and adapt their plans.

PEOPLE MANAGEMENT – KEEP IT SIMPLE, STUPID

People Management that delivers improved performance and sustainable results is not complicated. It does not need magic, secrets or rigid processes. It is an approach that is logical, ethical, fair, open and respectful.

Successful People Management starts and continues with you. Read, learn, implement and develop the fundamentals of People Management as set out in this book and you will build a successful high performing team.

REFERENCES AND RESOURCES

CHAPTER ONE

Great Place to Work® Institute, Inc. [viewed 21 February 2015]. Available from: http://www.greatplacetowork.co.uk

JOHNSON, Spencer. Who Moved My Cheese: An Amazing Way to Deal With Change In Your work and In Your Life. New York: Putnam Adult, 1999.

SUN TZU. The Art Of War. New York: Classic Books International, 2009.

CHAPTER TWO

JURAN, Joseph M. The Non-Pareto Principle; Mea Culpa. New York: Quality Progress, 1975, May, pp. 8–9.

CHAPTER THREE

ELLIS, Albert, & HARPER, Robert A. A Guide to Rational Living. 3rd Ed. Chatsworth,CA: Wilshire Book Company, 1975.

GOLEMAN, Daniel. Emotional Intelligence: Why It Can Matter More Than IQ. 10th Ed. New York: Bantam Books, 2006.

Substituting Rational Thinking for Irrational Thoughts [online]. UC Irvine Libraries, 2007-2015 [viewed on 21 February 2015]. Available from: http://www.lib.uci.edu/quest/index.php?page=ellis

MAKIN, Peter J., COOPER, Cary L and COX, Charles J. Organizations and the Psychological Contract: Managing People at Work. Oxford: Blackwell Publishers, 1996.

MAYO, Elton. The Human Problems of an Industrial Civilization. New York: Macmillan, 1933.

SALOVEY, Peter, & MAYER, John. Emotional Intelligence. Imagination, cognition, and personality, 1990, 9(3), 185-211.

CHAPTER FOUR

ALLEN, Roger E. Winnie-The-Pooh on Management: In Which a Very Important Bear and His Friends Are Introduced to a Very Important Subject. Reprint Edition. New York: Penguin Books, 2011.

CUMMINGS, Thomas G. and WORLEY, Christopher G. Organization Development & Change. 9th Ed. Mason OH: Cengage Learning, 2008, pp. 89-92.

MAKIN, Peter J., COOPER, Cary L and COX, Charles J. Organizations and the Psychological Contract: Managing People at Work. Oxford: Blackwell Publishers, 1996.

MASLOW, Abraham H. A theory of human motivation. Psychological Review, 1943, 50(4), 370–96.

SCHEIN, Edward H. Organizational Psychology. 3rd Ed. Englewood Cliffs, New Jersey: Prentice Hall, 1980.

SENGE, Peter. The Fifth Discipline: The art and practice of the learning organization. 2nd Ed. London: Random House, 2006.

SUN TZU. The Art Of War. New York: Classic Books International, 2009.

CHAPTER FIVE

CHEUNG-JUDGE, Mee-Yan. and HOLBECHE, Linda. Organization Development: A practitioner's guide for OD and HR. London: Kogan Page, 2011.

Strategic Human Resource Management [online]. Chartered Institute of Personnel and Development, Revised 2013 [viewed on 20 February 2015]. Available from: http://www.cipd.co.uk/hr-resources/factsheets/strategic-human-resource-management

WEST, Michael A., GUTHRIE, James P., DAWSON, Jeremy F., BORRILL, Carol S and CARTER, Matthew. Reducing patient mortality in hospitals: the role of human resource management. Journal of Organizational Behavior, 2006, 7, 983–1002.

CHAPTER SIX

ARMSTRONG, Michael and TAYLOR, Stephen. Armstrong's Handbook of Human Resource Management Practice. 12th Ed. London: Kogan Page, 2012.

BELBIN, Meredith R. Management Teams: Why They Succeed or Fail. 3rd Ed. Oxford: Butterworth Heinemann, 2010.

The Myers Briggs Foundation [viewed 20 February 2015]. Available from: http://www.myersbriggs.org

PETER, Lawrence J and HULL, Raymond. The Peter Principle: Why Things Always Go Wrong. New York: William Morrow and Company, 1969, pp 8.

The British Psychological Society [viewed 20 February 2015]. Available from: http://ptc.bps.org.uk

TAYLOR, Stephen. Employee Resourcing, Institute of Personnel and Development). London. UK, 1998.

CHAPTER SEVEN

Chartered Institute of Personnel and Development [viewed on 20 February 2015]. Available from: http://www.cipd.co.uk

Equality and Human Rights Commission [viewed on 20 February 2015]. Available from: http://www.equalityhumanrights.com

PINK, Daniel H. Drive: The Surprising Truth About What Motivates Us. Edinburgh: Canongate Books Ltd, 2011.

The Puzzle of Motivation [online]. TED Conferences, LLC [viewed on 20 February 2015]. Available from: http://www.ted.com/talks/dan_pink_on_motivation

The Pensions Regulator [viewed on 20 February 2015]. Available from: http://www.thepensionsregulator.gov.uk/

RSA Animate – Drive [online]. The RSA [viewed on 20 February 2015]. Available from: https://www.thersa.org/discover/videos/rsa-animate/2010/04/rsa-animate---drive/

ROSE, Michael. Reward Management (HR Fundamentals). London: Kogan Page, 2014.

CHAPTER EIGHT

BUCKINGHAM, Marcus and COFFMAN, Curt. First, break all the rules: What the World's Greatest Managers Do Differently. London: Pocket Books, 2005.

MORRIS, Edward. Journal of the History of Collections [online]. Oxford University Press 1992 4 (2) 169-173 [viewed on 20 February 2015]. Available from: http://jhc.oxfordjournals.org/content/4/2/169. extract

PINK, Daniel H. Drive: The Surprising Truth About What Motivates Us. Edinburgh: Canongate Books Ltd, 2011.

RINGELMANN, Max. Recherches sur les moteurs animés: Travail de l'homme" [Research on animate sources of power: The work of man] [online], Annales de l'Institut National Agronomique, 2nd series, 1913, 12, 1-40 [viewed on 20 February 2015]. Available in French from: http://gallica.bnf.fr/ark:/12148/bpt6k54409695.image.f14. langEN.)

STEWART, Henry. The Happy Manifesto: Make Your Organization A Great Workplace – Now! London: Happy, 2011.

The Puzzle of Motivation [online]. TED Conferences, LLC [viewed on 20 February 2015]. Available from: http://www.ted.com/talks/dan_pink_on_motivation

CHAPTER NINE

HERZBERG, Frederick. The Motivation to Work. New York: John Wiley and Sons, 1959.

PINK, Daniel H. Drive: The Surprising Truth About What Motivates Us. Edinburgh: Canongate Books Ltd, 2011, pp. 67.

BLAIR Gerard. The Human Factor [online]. The University of Edinburgh [viewed on 20 February 2015]. Available from: http://www.see.ed.ac.uk/~gerard/Management/art6.html

The Puzzle of Motivation. TED Conferences, LLC [viewed on 20 February 2015]. Available from: http://www.ted.com/talks/dan_pink_on_motivation

CHAPTER TEN

LENCIONI, Patrick. Overcoming the Five Dysfunctions of a Team: A Field Guide for Leaders, Managers and Facilitators. San Francisco CA: Jossey-Bass, 2005.

TUCKMAN, Bruce W. 'Developmental sequence in small groups', Psychological Bulletin, 1965, 63, 384-399.